EARTH MAGIC,
SKY MAGIC

Earth Magic, Sky Magic

Native American Stories

NEW EDITION

Rosalind Kerven

CAMBRIDGE
UNIVERSITY PRESS

Cambridge Reading

General Editors
Richard Brown and Kate Ruttle

Consultant Editor
Jean Glasberg

PUBLISHED BY THE PRESS SYNDICATE OF THE UNIVERSITY OF CAMBRIDGE
The Pitt Building, Trumpington Street, Cambridge CB2 1RP, United Kingdom

CAMBRIDGE UNIVERSITY PRESS
The Edinburgh Building, Cambridge CB2 2RU, United Kingdom
40 West 20th Street, New York, NY 10011-4211, USA
10 Stamford Road, Oakleigh, Melbourne 3166, Australia

First published 1991
Reprinted 1991, 1992, 1996
This edition published 1999

Printed in the United Kingdom at the University Press, Cambridge

Typeset in Concorde

A catalogue record for this book is available from the British Library

ISBN 0 521 63525 X paperback

Map by Peter Simmonett
Cover illustration by Amanda Hall

Contents

For Louise Power

PART 1

PEOPLE OF
THE SKY

The Man Who
Met the Sun

There once lived a chief's daughter whose eyes smouldered and blazed with a terrible, wonderful secret. All the young men were entranced by her and begged her to marry them; yet she refused even the finest.

At last her father told her,

"Your mother is growing old and so am I. One day we will both die. If you do not take a husband, you will be lonely and friendless: you will have no children, and because of this, you might forget how to laugh. Tell us what is troubling you and why you will not marry."

"Three summers ago," she replied, "I was alone fetching water from the river, when suddenly I was overcome by a storm of brilliant golden light. The Sun was upon me! I could feel His presence, hot and strong like fire. I fell to the ground and lay still, letting His words sink into my heart.

" 'Girl,' He said, 'you belong to me. I claim you as my daughter!' Oh my true beloved father, I dare not disobey the will of that great god! For then He said, 'I forbid you to take a husband unless you can find a man strong enough to show me my own Sun sign.' Father, I do not know what this sign is! So I shall never dare to marry, for if I disobey the Sun, He will surely scorch us with His anger and send disaster to our people."

Then she wept bitterly and her father, the chief, looked grave.

"I am glad you have spoken of this at last," he said. "Though the Sun dazzles us with His mysteries, I am certain that everything He does has a purpose. Sun's Daughter, you are honoured indeed that He has chosen you! Be patient, and obey Him always. Meanwhile, we will wait and watch and hope."

Several moons passed. Then one day, while she was wandering sadly along the river bank, she felt a stranger's eyes upon her. She turned, and saw a young man dressed in rags. He was tall and strong, but his face was disfigured by an ugly scar.

As she gazed at him, she felt a strange stirring in her heart; she lowered her eyes, afraid.

The young man called a polite greeting and came forward.

"You must be the one!" he said. "Do they not call you Sun's Daughter?"

Sorrowfully she nodded.

"Then listen," he said, "for I swear I will tell no lies. I am so poor that I must beg my way from camp to camp. I have no family and nothing to offer you. But I long to love you! I am not afraid to seek out the Sun Himself and ask Him for the sign that will release you to become my wife. So tell me: what do you say to this?"

She looked at him again, and a warm feeling rushed through her like snow-melt.

"If you go," she said, "I promise I will wait for you. Do not come back if you fail; but if you succeed, I shall be glad! I have learned to be patient. Know this, Scar Face: I will watch for you in hope."

So Scar Face left her; but he was afraid of what he must do.

He passed out of Sun Daughter's camp; and at that moment an old woman with deep eyes came from the darkness of her tipi, beckoning him inside.

"Stranger, you are in trouble," she said. "Speak of it, for I know many things and am always glad to offer help."

Scar Face sighed.

"I must make a long and dangerous journey. I have no mother or wife or sister to cook me food. I have no father or uncle or older brother to offer good advice."

The wise woman looked at him long and carefully.

"I will give you some gifts to help you on your way," she said. "Firstly, here are seven pairs of moccasins to make you sure-footed as the deer. Secondly, here is a sack of meat and corn to give you strength. Thirdly, I offer you this handful of wisdom:

Follow the path that the Sun Himself will show you.

Take the help of any creature that will give it.

But do not take anything which does not belong to you."

Scar Face thanked her warmly. Then he set out along the path she pointed to, towards the setting Sun.

For countless days and moons he walked. He crossed the prairie. He climbed steep hills and tramped down through lonely, echoing valleys. He finished all his food and wore out all his moccasins. Now a dark, mysterious forest lay ahead.

Lost and weary, he sank to rest amongst the roots and leaves, praying for some helper to come along.

Very soon, a wolf came padding up.

"Greetings my brother. What are you doing so far from home?"

"Oh brother Wolf," said Scar Face, "I am seeking the mighty Sun, for only He can give me what I long for. But I cannot find the way."

The wolf shook his head.

"Alas, I have never seen that great god's house. But do not despair, for Bear is very wise. He may guide you."

Scar Face thanked him and followed the sound of rumbling snores to a great cave.

"Brother Bear, are you at home?" he called.

The bear came yawning out.

"What do you want of me?"

"I want to know the road to the Sun's house," said Scar Face, and he told the bear his story.

"Ah," said the bear, "I have never seen it. But over there is the badger's hole: he may know."

Scar Face thanked him and went whispering down the badger's hole,

"Help me please, brother Badger! Tell me the road to the Sun!"

The badger blinked out at him.

"Brother Man, I can tell you nothing. But ask the wolverine, for he knows every inch of forest and mountains, and has been right to the world's edge."

So Scar Face thanked him and ran onwards, calling,

"Where are you, Wolverine my brother? And where is the road to the Sun?"

Above him, in the tangled branches, the wolverine's face looked down, a gleam of eyes and teeth.

"Night is falling," he said. "Be patient. Wait until morning; then I will gladly show you."

At dawn, the wolverine took Scar Face down a narrow track, very overgrown and gloomy. At its far end, the wolverine slunk away, leaving Scar Face alone on the edge of a Great Water. It was grey and empty, restless with waves, flecked with foam, so vast that he could not see the far shore.

"It is too wide to swim across," he thought, "and even if I had strength left to build a canoe, it would not survive those crashing waves. Now I know that my quest is truly hopeless."

But at that moment, two white swans came swimming up.

"Why are you waiting here?" they called.

"I wait here in shame," replied Scar Face, "because I have failed to finish what I began – to find the house of the Sun."

"*Kyi!*" cried the swans. "You have not failed! Beyond this water lies the Sky, and that is where the Sun lives. Brother, let us carry you there!"

So Scar Face rode on the swans' backs. The journey was long and stormy, the water wild with writhing shadows. But the swans swam steadily until they reached the other side.

"The Sun's trail leads from this beach," they said.

Scar Face thanked them and set out along a broad, bright path.

Suddenly he found his way blocked by a pile of treasures: a war-shirt, a shield, a bow and a quiver full of arrows, each one exquisitely worked. Scar Face gazed at them longingly; but he did not take or even touch them, remembering the wise woman's words.

He walked a little further, and soon he met a handsome youth wrapped in a robe of strange furs. His skin was red and on his head he wore a red eagle's feather.

"Greetings," said the red one. "There were some weapons back along the path. I expected to see you carrying them."

"I did not touch them," replied Scar Face, "for they are not mine."

"No," said the red youth, "but they are mine. It is well that you are honest! So – tell me your name and why you have travelled all this way to the Sky."

"My name is Scar Face. I have come here to speak with the Sun."

The red youth smiled.

"Well then, you are lucky! I am Morning Star and the Sun is my father. Come with me: when night falls you shall meet the one you seek."

He led Scar Face to a huge wooden lodge, painted all over with magic birds, beasts and patterns. Inside, a pale, shining woman sat upon a shimmering blanket.

"This is my mother, the Moon," said Morning Star. Then to the woman he said, "This man wishes to see my father."

The Moon smiled and nodded.

Soon they heard rumbling footsteps, the lodge filled with light and the Sun Himself came dazzling in through the doorway.

"Be still!" he cried. "Who is there? I smell a person!"

"Father," said Morning Star, "the one we expected has come."

The Sun fixed His golden eyes on Scar Face.

"You are welcome indeed," he said. "Everything is as it should be. Do not ask anything of me yet; but be our guest and a friend to our son."

The next day Morning Star asked Scar Face to go hunting with him. As they were setting out, the Moon called Scar Face to her and whispered.

"Keep my son well away from the Great Water! For terrible, evil monsters live there. Once Morning Star had many brothers, but one by one the monsters have killed them all. Because of this, we are often sad and lonely."

"I shall take good care of him," promised Scar Face.

For a long time he stayed with them, an honoured guest. Each day he went hunting with Morning Star, and together they filled the Sun's lodge with meat.

But one day they could not find any more game. Morning Star led the way down many secret trails, searching and searching but always in vain. Suddenly, emerging from a dry, stony gulley, they found themselves where they should not be: on the edge of the Great Water!

"I see a deer!" cried Morning Star; and at once he went running down after a dark, leaping shadow that flashed along the shore.

"No, no, keep away!" Scar Face shouted after him; but the red youth was already on the water's edge.

Too late, the shadow revealed itself as a monster! *Shuckk! Sleeeth! Yaagh!* Evil claws and teeth came clutching! Morning Star stood bewitched, unable to fight or flee.

But Scar Face crept after him along the ground, where the monster could not see him. He hid in dust-holes, behind bushes and boulders, until he was close enough to aim his bow.

His arrows flew with skill and swiftness.

Yaagh! Yaagh! The monster shrieked and scratched the air. *Aarrackk!* Then all was quiet and still.

Morning Star woke from his trance. He saw the evil creature lying dead; he saw Scar Face with an empty quiver.

"You have saved me!" he said. "Come, we must go and tell my father."

It was evening when they reached the lodge. The Moon was out, but the Sun sat there in all His splendour.

"Father," cried Morning Star, "Scar Face has saved my life!" He told the story of the monster. "Now he is truly my brother."

"That is so," said the Sun, "and to me, Scar Face, you are like a son. You must take a gift from your new father. Tell me what you would like."

"There is only one thing that I long for," said Scar Face, "and that is to marry the young woman whom you once claimed as a daughter. I have asked her, and she is willing."

The Sun nodded. "I have watched her for a long time. She has carried her burden patiently and her heart has always been pure and strong. And I have watched you, my son. You have wandered far to find me. You have always kept to the path, though the way was often hard. You have risked everything to prove your love.

"Return to Earth and go to her. Tell her that I myself have sent you. But wait: let her know it is true by this sign."

Then the Sun came to Scar Face and rubbed one of His golden hands across his cheek. For a brief moment, Scar Face's whole body trembled with light. Then it was over; and when he put up his own hand to feel, the scar was gone.

"Now," said the Sun, "I will give you another precious gift, and that is wisdom. Understand these things: the Great Mystery shines through me. I made the world, the animals, the people. I can never die. I alone am your chief.

"Wear the raven's feathers, for he is clever. Eat the buffalo's meat, for he is sacred. Tell your people always to do good, then I will take pity on them in their troubles.

"But now it is time for you to go."

The Sun and Morning Star gave Scar Face many wonderful presents: shirts and leggings, moccasins, bags and blankets. Then the Moon came in from her night-time journey, and wept when she heard that Scar Face was leaving, until the floor was covered in her blue, shining tears.

The Sun took Scar Face out to the edge of the Sky. They looked down and saw the great Earth below them, slumbering in all its beauty.

"Look where the stars show thick and white against the night," He said. "That is the Wolf Road, or the Milky Way. Follow where it leads until you reach your journey's end."

Scar Face could not find words to thank Him. But the Sun smiled kindly saying, "I know all things within your heart. You do not need to tell me. I am always with you."

So Scar Face set off down the Wolf Road. His head was filled with singing and his heart was filled with light.

It was high summer when Scar Face came back to the camp, and very hot. All the people were resting in the shade; but he stopped a short way off, in the full heat of the Sun.

After a while, Sun's Daughter noticed him. Thinking he was a stranger, she went out to offer him a cooling drink.

Scar Face saw her coming and hid his face in his robe.

"Does the Sun not burn you stranger?" she asked.

"A father does not harm his son," replied Scar Face. "And to you I am no stranger!"

Then he threw back his robe, and she saw who it was.

"You have come back!"

"It was a long way," said Scar Face quietly, "and more than once I nearly died. But I found the Sun and did what I must for Him. He has sent me back home to you: look, he has taken away my scar, as His sign."

"It was a long time," whispered Sun's Daughter, "and more than once, I too nearly died. But now the great test is really over!"

Thus they married; and words cannot tell of the happiness that came to them. The Sun sent them blessings of peace and fruitfulness; and the Great Mystery's pure light shone from both their eyes.

Moon-Woman and the
Arrow-Chain Boy

There were two boys who had practised with bow and arrows until they were the best shooters in the land. Then they grew proud: too proud, arrogant; they feared no-one and nothing, not even the realm of spirits.

It happened that one night they went shooting together on top of a lonely hill. As they practised, they talked and joked.

"Hey!" said the first. "Just look at the Moon up there! Isn't it ugly? It's got scars and spots all over its face!"

With these words, he fitted another arrow to his bow and shot it . . . wooosh! . . . up, up, straight to the Moon.

The two boys laughed out loud together. But at that very moment, the Moon disappeared and so did all the stars. Now it was dark, dark, absolute, complete.

A shimmering ring of rainbow-light appeared. Here, there, it darted as if it were searching, seeking, rooting something out. Then the second boy heard a shriek that made his blood freeze.

He held his breath. Slowly, slowly the rainbow-ring faded; slowly the stars winked back into the sky and the Moon sailed into view again from behind a bank of clouds.

But the first boy had gone!

"Hey, hey, where are you?" cried the other; but deep in his heart he already knew. His friend had been stolen away by the Moon! It was a punishment for their mockery, for shouting out such insults.

For a long time, the second boy sat very still, thinking. He could not go back to the village alone. He who had no fear of anything: he must go after his friend and rescue him.

So he took his bow and shot a second arrow into the Sky.

This time, he was careful. This arrow did not touch the Moon, it did not

16

touch the stars. But it stuck tight to the darkness, and hung there where he could clearly see it. Then he shot another arrow up, and another and another and another, until his quiver was completely empty. The arrows hung down from the Sky in a long, long chain, and the last one touched the Earth.

He put his ear to the bottom of the arrow-chain. Far, far away he could hear his friend crying piteously, moaning and groaning.

He stopped to think, to make plans.

First he walked all round the hill. Every time he came to a bush with edible berries growing on it, he broke off a branch and stuck it into his hair.

Then he tied a long rope around his waist.

By the time he was ready, day had broken. He climbed the arrow-chain: up . . . up . . . up.

Soon he felt hungry. He stopped and reached into his hair. One of the branches had grown heavy with fruit. He pulled off a big bunch of red berries and ate them. When he had finished, he went on climbing.

After a time, he grew tired. He tied the ends of the rope round his waist to the arrow-chain: now he could let go without falling off. Then he closed his eyes and went to sleep, rocked by the gentle wind.

In this way he climbed for two days and two nights until at long last he reached the Sky.

It was still dark and he was very weary, so he stepped off the arrow-chain, lay down and slept.

But he could not rest long, for suddenly someone was shaking him awake. Opening his eyes, he saw a young girl standing next to him.

"Hey, get up sleepy-head," she smiled. "My grandmother is waiting."

The boy followed her through the dark trails of the Sky world to a small house. Inside sat an old woman whose eyes winked and twinkled with starlight.

"Ho! Come in, come in!" she called. "So, you have come looking for your friend, eh? At least you are as brave as you are rude and foolish. Well, it's no secret: Moon-Woman stole him and made him her slave, for she doesn't like being laughed at. She's my neighbour: she lives just down that track – it's not very far. But if you want to rescue him, you must do it all by yourself."

The boy nodded. "I am not afraid," he said, "but I am hungry."

17

"Then we shall feed you," said the kind old grandmother, "and then I shall try to find four gifts which might be of some help."

While she spoke, the girl had slipped out to fetch bowls piled high with delicious salmon and seal-meat. They ate; but the meal was disturbed by distant sounds of crying and screaming.

"Ah, that is your friend," said the kind old grandmother, shaking her head. "Moon-Woman hates him. She beats him and treats him most cruelly."

When they had finished, the kind old grandmother shuffled around the house looking for things. She gave the Arrow-Chain Boy a huge pine-cone, a piece of tree-root, a spray of roses and a fragment of stone.

"Each of these has magic within it," she said, "but you must work out for yourself how to use it. If you succeed and bring your friend here safely, I will show you how to get home."

The boy thanked her and went out. The first thing he saw was Moon-Woman's house, shimmering with silver light in the distance.

He crept up to it, he circled it silently, round and round, always watching, always listening. He could hear his friend's screams quite clearly now, coming from high up in the roof near the smoke-hole.

Still watching, still listening, he made a plan.

First, he knocked on the door. But before Moon-Woman could open it, he ran away and jumped up onto the roof.

He saw Moon-Woman open the door, watched her turn her white, blotchy face this way, that way; heard her shrieking,

"Who's there? Who's there? Ai-eee, when I catch you, you'll be sorry!"

Then he slipped down the smoke-hole.

His friend was there, lying on the cross-beam, tied up tightly with ropes.

Quickly he cut him free.

"Oh, it's good to see you!"

"Yes, and you! Listen, I have magic to help us get away."

The Arrow-Chain Boy felt in his clothes, and the first thing he found was the pine-cone. Carefully he put it on the beam where his friend had been bound. At once the cone began to sigh and scream, sounding just like a captured boy. Concealed by its noise, the two boys climbed out onto the roof, jumped down and started to run.

At that very moment, Moon-Woman came back.

"Ooo-loooh!" she cackled, "they are trying to fool me!"

She heard the pine-cone sighing and screaming.

"Tricks and teasing! Ooo-loooh, how I shall beat them both!" cried Moon-Woman. She poked about the beams with a long stick, and the cone tumbled down to the ground and lay still, in shameful silence.

Then she opened the door and gave chase.

It was not far back to the kind old grandmother's house. The two boys ran and ran. As they went, the Arrow-Chain Boy threw down the piece of tree-root. At once it grew into a thicket of towering trees, rooted between Moon-Woman and themselves.

But Moon-Woman was strong, Moon-Woman was angry. She fought and struggled through the thicket and soon she had passed right through.

Now she was gaining on the boys again and it looked as if she might catch them!

On and on they went. This time the Arrow-Chain Boy threw down the spray of roses behind him. At once it grew into a great, tangled fence of sweet-smelling thorns.

But Moon-Woman could take any pain. Moon-Woman would not be beaten. She plunged straight through the prickles. Now she was almost treading on their heels!

The Arrow-Chain Boy glanced behind and threw back the fragment of stone. It landed at Moon-Woman's feet. At once it grew into an enormous cliff with sides as smooth and slippery as ice. Moon-Woman gave a cackle of fury and tried to climb up. But she was like a round, white ball: she just kept rolling back and back and back . . .

So at last the two boys reached the kind old grandmother's house. They were safe!

"Good, good," she greeted them. "Now you must go at once with my granddaughter. She will take you back to the place where your arrow-chain first entered the Sky. When you get there, think of nothing but your home. Keep thinking of it until you arrive there."

The girl led them back to the arrow-chain and said goodbye.

The boys sat there, still and quiet; they thought of home. Soon they began to float down, down through the air. But it was hard to concentrate: every so often one of them remembered their strange Sky adventure, and then they bounced straight back and had to start again.

But at last they managed it. They thought and thought and thought. Oh wonders! . . . they found themselves back on the firm ground of their own village.

Well, their parents were overjoyed to see them again! They had just been getting ready for a big funeral feast because they had thought the boys were dead. As soon as they saw them alive and well, they turned it into a celebration!

Star Sister,
Star Brothers

The Quillwork Girl had nimble fingers that seemed to be touched with magic. All day long she sat sewing exquisite patterns made from brightly dyed porcupine quills onto tipi-skins, quivers and robes. It was said that dreams flashed like sunlight before her eyes: she could decorate things more beautifully than anyone else in the world.

One day her mother came saying,

"What are you making now, my daughter?"

The girl looked up. Her smile was soft and far, far away.

"I am making seven shirts, Mother, to go with these seven pairs of leggings and seven pairs of moccasins."

"But who are they for, my daughter? Your father is dead. You have no brothers. Your uncles and your boy-cousins have wives and sisters of their own to sew their clothes. Can it be that there are seven young men courting you who need such gifts?"

The girl laughed.

"I don't know who they are for. But I have dreamed that I must make them. Perhaps I will know when they are finished."

So she sewed and sewed for many days.

When the garments were ready, she told her mother,

"My work is done and I am leaving now to deliver my seven gifts."

"But where are you going, my daughter?"

"Towards the North, towards the land of snow."

"And who will you give your gifts to, my daughter?"

"To my lost brothers, far away, who are waiting."

Then the mother began to weep: "If you go, my only child, then I shall never see you or your lovely handiwork again."

But the Quillwork Girl shook her head.

"That is not so. One day, Mother, you will see me in the Sky. I will smile and you will know me. Then the whole world will be able to admire my work!"

With these words, she went out through the village, collecting from her neighbours seven strong dogs. She wrapped up the clothes she had made into seven bundles and strapped each bundle to a dog. Then, driving the animals before her, she set out on her long journey to the North.

For many, many days she wandered, meeting no-one. Then one evening she came to a big, lonely tipi on the far side of a stream.

"Hoo, hoo, hoo!" she called. "Here I come, the Quillwork Girl, looking for seven who will make me their sister!"

At once, the tipi door burst open and a young boy stepped out smiling.

"Welcome!" he said. "We have been expecting you. My six older brothers are all out hunting, but they will be back soon. There is plenty to eat: every day they bring back extra meat, in the hope that you might come."

The Quillwork Girl unloaded her bundles and sent the dogs home, as a sign to her mother that she was safe and had arrived. Then she waded across the stream and entered her new home.

How glad the other six were when they returned to find her! They cooked her a wonderful feast of fresh-killed venison and exclaimed with joy over the beautiful clothes she had made them.

And so they settled down to live happily together, like any family. But alas, everything in the world must change . . .

One day the Quillwork Girl was alone in the tipi. She heard a scratching and stepped out to investigate. There stood a milk-white buffalo calf, waiting to talk.

"What do you want?" asked the girl.

"I have a message from my father," said the milk-white calf. "He is the Chief of all the Buffalo. He has seen the beautiful things you can make: he wants you! You must come and live with us and work for the Buffalo Chief."

"No!" said the girl. "I am of the People, not of the Buffalo. I belong here with my seven new brothers. I will never go with you!"

So the milk-white calf went away.

When her brothers came home, the Quillwork Girl told them what had happened.

"Let us wait and see," she said. "I am not afraid."

But now every day they left the youngest brother at home to wait with her.

Three days passed in peace. But on the fourth morning the girl and the boy saw the side of the tipi billowing in and out as if some large creature were charging it.

This time the boy stepped outside. There he found an enormous buffalo cow stamping the ground with impatience.

"Where is she?" bellowed the cow. "My husband is calling for her! No-one may ignore his summons for he is the Chief of all the Buffalo! She must come and live with us, she must come and work for the Buffalo Chief!"

"No!" said the boy. "She is of the People, not of the Buffalo. She is our new sister and belongs here with us. She will never go with you!"

"Then the Chief himself will come," roared the cow. "Let me warn you about him. He is bigger than the mountains. He is fiercer than fire. He will kill you all if the Quillwork Girl does not give herself up!"

Then the buffalo cow went away.

When the six young men came home, their youngest brother told them what had happened. They were all very worried.

Yet still the Quillwork Girl said, "Let us wait and see. I am not afraid."

But now all seven brothers gave up their hunting. They lived on dried meat and stayed at home to wait with her.

Three more days passed in peace. But on the fourth morning the ground beneath their tipi began to shudder and tremble as if there were about to be an earthquake. Then suddenly they heard a roaring, seven times louder than thunder. The walls of the tipi were ripped away. There he stood, snorting flames before them: the mighty Buffalo Chief!

"Where is she?" he bellowed. "Give her to me – NOW!"

The Quillwork Girl and the six older brothers were all very afraid. But the youngest boy stood his ground before the mighty buffalo and laughed up into his face.

"You will never catch her!" he cried. "You will never touch any of us. For I know magic that will carry us to the Sky!"

Then he turned to his sister and brothers.

"Quick! Behind you is a tree. Jump into its branches and hold on tight!"

They all did as he told them.

As soon as they were up, the boy took his bow and shot an arrow into its trunk. Then he leaped up beside them.

At once the tree began to grow: *zipp . . . zippp! . . .* carrying the girl and her brothers far beyond the reach of the angry Buffalo Chief.

"HAAARR!" With a roar such as the world had never heard before, the Buffalo Chief charged at the tree.

"I will chop it down with my horns!" he yelled. "Then I will seize the Quillwork Girl and kill all the rest!"

The girl and the six older brothers all shrieked with terror. But the youngest boy laughed down at the buffalo and shot another arrow into the top of the trunk.

At once it grew even taller, carrying the girl and her brothers higher, higher to safety.

"HAAR–AAR–AAR!"

The Buffalo Chief charged again. This time his mighty horns sliced a huge gash halfway through the tree.

The youngest boy had a single arrow left. He shot it into the uppermost branches. For the last time, his magic made the tree grow again, carrying the family high above the clouds.

They heard the Buffalo Chief charge; they saw the tree shake, wobble, topple right over.

But the Quillwork Girl and her seven brothers were safe for ever. For at that very moment they stepped off and walked away into the Sky!

Now the beautiful clothes they wore began to glow with strange, translucent light.

The girl looked down at the Earth.

"Mother," she called, "can you see me? Look, my handiwork is up here for all the world to admire until the end of time!"

Far, far below, the mother knew in her heart that her daughter was calling. She stepped out of her tipi and gazed up at the night.

There in the black Sky she saw a new constellation of eight stars.

Tonight, you too might see them if you look. The seven brothers shine in the shape of what the White People call 'The Plough'. They are all pointing to one brilliant, twinkling star that never moves. The White People call it the 'North Star' or the 'Pole Star'; but *we* know that it is really the Quillwork Girl shining in all her glory.

Flying
with the Thunders

There was a youth who went out hunting in the mountains. He got lost as the darkness drew in and fell down a deep, dark ravine.

"Help!" he screamed, "I will surely die!"

Indeed, the fall was long and terrible, but he landed softly: broken but not dead. For many hours he lay unconscious in that gloomy cleft; then finally he awoke.

Through his pain he heard a voice and saw a cave gaping dark in the rock behind him. Before it sat an old, old man with white hair flowing down to his waist.

"Where am I? Who are you?"

"Ah, you have fallen to my home like a gift from the Sky," said the old man hoarsely. "Never mind who I am. I can help you – but I might not want to. We could strike a bargain – but *you* might not want to. This is it: I will heal you, nurse you and make you well again. But after that you must stay here with me and be my slave!"

He gave a cruel laugh. "That's a fine one, eh, a fine one, isn't it?! On the other hand, if you prefer freedom, my friend, you are quite free to stay here, untouched, until you die."

The youth was like all creatures: he wanted to live. So he let the old man heal him.

When he was well and could walk and run again, he settled down to keep his side of the bargain.

The old man was a cruel slave-master. Every day he sent the youth out hunting; and the meat he caught, all of it, was to be brought straight back to him, untouched. Then the youth had to butcher it and cook it; but he had nothing to eat himself, except for meagre scraps of gristle that the old man threw him as if he were a dog. At night he was kept busy with an endless string of petty tasks, before being allowed to curl up for a brief sleep, far from the warmth of the fire.

Yet he thought: I have survived death. Nothing else can hurt me now. Freedom will surely come.

Autumn and winter passed in this way; and then it was spring.

"Go and catch me a bear to eat," said the old man. "No matter how long it takes, do not come back without it."

So the youth searched and followed huge footprints away through the mud, far, far beyond the ravine, to the edge of a deep, thick forest.

He caught the bear and killed it, but before he could start for home, he was stopped by a deep rumble of urgent voices calling:

"Wait! Bring him out of the darkness!"

The youth whirled round. Four big men stood there, watching him. Their skin was damp with dew. Their robes were vaguely drifting, vaporous robes, like clouds.

"What . . .?! Who are you?"

"We are the Thunders," they said. "We soar from Sky to Earth, from Earth to Sky. We watch, here, there, everything, everywhere. We bring rain, we nurture life. We root out evil, we punish and destroy."

"What do you want of me?"

The Thunders touched him with grey, transparent hands.

"We want the Old Man of the Ravine. We want to burn up his evil! He feeds on slaves, just as a spider catches flies. He is older than the cedar trees: long before you were born, hundreds of innocent people had already been worked to skin and bones by him and eaten alive! So long as he shelters in the magic darkness of his cave, we cannot touch him. You alone have the chance to bring him out to us . . . Then we shall shrivel him up with our anger!"

The youth was afraid: more afraid of the Thunders even than of his cruel master. So, promising to help, he hurried back to the ravine.

"Master!" he called. "I found a bear. It is huge and its meat is rich with fat, but . . ."

The old man hobbled out, prodding the youth with a sharp stick.

"Where is it? How dare you come back empty-handed, slave."

"Master, it is too heavy – impossible – for me to carry alone. You must come, you must help me."

The old man began to shake with outrage. "How dare you? I cannot leave my shelter: it is too dangerous." But saliva dribbled from his twisted mouth at the thought of the good meat.

"Master," begged the youth, "the crows will steal it if we delay."

"Oh, very well, very well, I will come and help you. But afterwards, you can be sure you will suffer!" He glanced nervously at the sky. "And we must be back well before it rains!"

The old man followed the youth along the bear's trail; but all the time he was shivering.

"I can feel storm clouds gathering," he grumbled. "They smell of death. Wait, wait while I sharpen my magic." Then he sniffed the distance and began to dribble again. "But hurry, hurry, we must not lose it!"

Many times they stopped and faltered; but at last the old man saw the bear. Smacking his lips, he broke into a run.

At that very moment, the clouds burst and rain blanketed down.

The old man shrieked, he jerked; and then he started to spin. Round and round and round he went, chanting a weird song, faster and faster, until words and body were blurred and lost . . .

The rain parted and the Thunders stepped out. Lightning flashed from their fingers.

But the old man had turned himself into a porcupine!

He plucked quills from himself, spat poison onto them and shot them full in the faces of the Thunders.

They sent the poisoned quills back to him, rumbling with echoes of bitter laughter. Then, with a single mighty lightning bolt, they struck the old man dead!

The youth bowed his head humbly before them.

"You have made me free as the wind again," he whispered. "How can I ever thank you? I must do something for you in return."

"Your time will come," they said. "Keep patient, as you have been. Do right to everyone, and you will be happy."

Then the Thunders broke off fragments of their own cloud robes and draped them over his shoulders. They felt full of light and air. When he moved his arms inside them, he rose from the ground like a winged bird.

"These robes will carry you home again," they said. "When you get there, hide them, live well and wait for us."

So the youth did as they told him. He flew home. His mother cried with joy to see him. He hid the cloud robes and kept the secret of his adventure close to his heart.

Thus, in peace, the year turned. Spring peeled open again. The first rains fell; and under dark clouds, the Thunders came to fetch him.

"Fly with us!" they roared. "Keep your promise! Hunt with us from Sky to Earth, from Earth to Sky, until we have struck down every shoot of this year's evil!"

So all through the spring rains, he went flying with the Thunders. They looked for cruel men, for quarrelsome women; they sought out cheats and traitors and liars. Oh, it was a terrible thing to be guilty and struck down with their thunderbolts! But in their wake, the air cleared, butterflies danced and the new growth pushed through, green and strong.

The third new moon of the season was growing big when the Thunders spoke:

"Everything is done, except for one thing. The Great Grub still lives and lurks. He poisons and ruins the crops; he spreads hunger through the world. We cannot finish, we cannot leave until this last one is rooted out."

When he heard this, the youth sighed with weariness. He longed to go home, but the Thunders would not release him until everything was complete.

Silently, sadly, he dropped to Earth to drink from a lonely pool. But when he flew back into the Sky, the Thunders all turned upon him.

"Where have you been?" they roared. "There is foul oil on your lips! It smells like the poisonous spittle of the Great Grub!"

The youth trembled to think that they doubted his trust.

"Mighty Thunders, I swear I did not know! Follow me and I will lead you straight back to the place where it comes from."

He took them to the pool. The Thunders encircled it: one to the North, one to the South, one to the East, one to the West. They linked arms and, with a single breath, released four gigantic thunderbolts.

The waters of the lake burst and frothed up into a geyser; then they gushed away. In the hollow where they had been, a huge, ugly, oozing maggot lay curled up, dead.

"Thus we are finished," said the Thunders. "Go back to your village now, and stay there. Remember this promise: if your people dig the ground each spring, and their hearts are pure, we will send lightning to kill the grubs that eat their crops, and rain to make them strong."

For the last time, the youth flew. He went straight home. Then the cloud robes fell from his shoulders and dissolved away like morning mist.

When his story was told and understood, everyone stopped fearing the Thunders. Since then, the People have honoured them.

The Big
Snow

All this happened long, long ago – so far back that people had not yet been created. Things were fine then! The animals and birds that shared the world lived together in complete peace and friendship. They all loved and looked after the Earth. They ate no living flesh: nothing but shoots and leaves, roots and berries. Everyone spoke the same language. There was no killing, no fighting, not even any arguments.

But good times never last for ever. One night it grew so dark that the animals could not even see their own paws. Then it began to snow, layer upon layer, until everything was covered, lost. The birds were all grounded in the blizzard.

At last, everyone managed to tunnel their way through and meet together for a council.

"Something terrible is going on," they agreed. "The creatures up in the Sky World are playing nasty tricks on us. We'll have to visit them up there, try to sort out the trouble."

So as soon as the blizzard had eased, all the birds flew up, up, up to the great trap-door that separates the Earth from the Sky; and on their backs they carried all the animals.

They passed through the trap-door. On the other side, the first thing that they saw was a large lake; and on its banks, an enormous lodge with walls made of deer-hide.

"Just look!" shrieked Deer, "what kind of place have we come to, where the skins of my dead sisters and brothers are used to build houses?"

Nevertheless, they all swallowed their horror and went inside. There they found three small bear cubs.

"Go away!" cried the cubs. "What do you want? Our mother is out."

Fox drew himself up, straight and tall. He spoke with a chief's authority in his voice:

"You must tell us where she is."

"She is hunting," replied the cubs.

"Hunting? What is hunting?"

"It is chasing," said the cubs, "and killing."

A gasp of shock ran through all the Earth creatures.

"Killing is wrong," said Fox severely. "Killing is evil. What is the purpose of your mother committing this crime?"

Then the little bear cubs began to look very frightened. "Please, please, we know nothing except for what our mother taught us. She promised to hunt a caribou. She will bring back its meat for us to eat. We didn't know that it's wrong to be hungry . . ."

At the back of the crowd of Earth creatures, Caribou was sobbing. But Mouse strode forward and silenced him with an urgent squeak.

"Hush! This is no time to feel sorry for ourselves. We have trouble to overcome: we must rid Earth of the Big Snow. I believe that the answer lies within this lodge."

She began to scurry about searching, up and down, here and there. Suddenly her black eye rested upon five bulging bags that hung down from the cross-beams of the ceiling.

"Tell me: what are those?" she asked the cubs.

"Leave them! They are secret!" The cubs were all trembling and squealing. "Our mother has set us here to guard them. Some dreadful catastrophe will happen if they are broken or even touched!"

"What is in them, what is in them?" roared all the animals, squawked all the birds, at once.

"We shan't tell you – we *can't* tell you! You must wait for our mother to come back!"

"If you don't tell us – now – then I shall gnaw a great big hole in each one," threatened Mouse. "Then we will find out for ourselves exactly what this dreadful catastrophe is."

At this, the little bears became beside themselves with panic.

"No, no, don't touch!" they cried. "All right, we'll tell you. This one contains the Winds! The second contains the Rain! The third contains the Cold! The fourth contains the Fog! . . . There! Now go away and leave us alone!"

"But there are *five* bags altogether," said Fox quietly. "What is in the last one?"

"We shall *never* give that away. It's a terrible, dangerous, magical secret! . . . Oh, but listen, listen: there is the sound of our mother's canoe coming into the shore!"

"My guess is that this last bag is the one that we must obtain," Fox whispered to Mouse.

"Yes indeed," she agreed. "Just now my ears tell me it is true: outside, I hear the big Bear herself coming; so the first thing we must do is hide."

At this, all the animals and birds slipped out of the lodge and into the tall fir trees that surrounded it. There in the dark green shadows they hid; and as they waited they worked out a plan.

First, Fox went back into the lodge.

"Your mother is almost here," he told the cubs, "but her sack is empty. She sends this message for you: If you want to eat meat tonight, you must help her. Look out for Caribou running past, and give her a shout when you see him."

Next, Mouse slipped out of the trees and into the lapping water of the lake. *Swish-swash, swish-swash* . . . along came Mother Bear, swiftly paddling her canoe.

Mouse swam right up to her. She jumped unseen onto the paddle. With her small, sharp teeth she nibbled and gnawed a cut, deep and clean through the handle.

Then Mouse flicked her tail: a signal to Caribou. Caribou jumped into the lake, swam ashore in full view of the bears' lodge, and ran into the woods.

The three cubs spotted him and ran outside shouting:

"Mother, Mother, there he goes: caribou flees into the trees!"

Mother Bear heard and saw. She began to paddle faster, faster. But remember Mouse's good work, gnawing. Suddenly the handle of the paddle snapped – *crack!* – clean in two. The canoe wobbled and capsized.

Bear was hurled into the water – down, down, right to the cold, dark bottom!

The cubs ran to the shore, crying and screaming, calling for their mother. It was piteous to hear them, but the Earth creatures had no time for pity. As soon as the way was clear, they burst back into the lodge.

"Seize the fifth bag!" yelled Fox.

Mouse scurried up and gnawed through the rope that held it. At once the bag, bulging with secrets, tumbled into Fox's outstretched paws.

He pulled open the strings. Light burst out, warm and brilliant. It was the Sun, the Moon, the Stars!

"This is what we need: this is what will break the winter!"

The birds caught them all in their beaks. They flew with them to the Sky trap-door and pushed them out, down towards the Earth.

Soft and golden, warmly, gently, the Sun, the Moon, the Stars drifted across that blue place that lies between Earth and Sky.

And the Big Snow melted. Peering down, the Earth creatures saw spring unfold itself, the rivers flow again, the Earth turn green.

One by one, the birds and animals dropped down through the trap-door. Singing under the warm sunshine, happily, they went home.

PART 2

SPIDER WOMAN

In the
Beginning

Tell me: what was it like right in the beginning, when the world was new?

It was dark, my child, and our people were lost: deep, deep under the ground.

How did they get out? How did they come to live here, under the yellow sun and the blue sky?

Mole led them.

Mole?

Yes. He dug the way up, up and out. The People followed him up through the long tunnel until they emerged right out of the darkness. They stood there on the beautiful bright Earth, but the light dazzled them and hurt their eyes. They were so afraid that they wanted to run back into the darkness and hide!

What stopped them?

A voice.

Whose voice? What did it say?

It was sweet and fluting, the voice of an old, old woman. It said, "Wait! I will help you." And then, "Cover your eyes, once, twice, three times, four times; then look and you will be able to see me." They did as she told them. And indeed, there she was: Spider Woman!

Was it really her? What did she look like?

Oh . . . my child, she was . . . small and dark, wrinkled. She was sweet and warm, like her voice.

"I am your grandmother," she said. "I was old before the Sun was born. I am the grandmother of the Earth, and of all living things."

From within the lost shadows of her ancient body, she began to spin an endless thread of silk.

"This is my wisdom," she said. "Do not quarrel, do not fight, do not make wars. Take care of all things that grow and the Earth that feeds them. Do you want to be happy, my grandchildren? Then you must not hurt anyone, or anything, ever, in any way."

What happened then?

She sent the People away to find their home. They wandered East, North, West and South until at last they came here, to the Middle Land. They built marvellous towns and villages of mud and rock. They grew fine crops of corn. They lived well.

And were they happy?

Ah child, look around you: *is* everyone happy?

I don't... No, not everyone. Often many people seem to look sad.

And why is that, do you think?

Is it because... well, they have not really remembered the things that Spider Woman taught them?

Exactly, exactly! People fight and quarrel, they hurt each other. And because of this, they know sorrow. Spider Woman watches us all and weeps so bitterly for our foolishness that her tears light the stars.

If only she could come back again! If only she was there to show us the way!

Ah, but she does, my child. She is often there to help. Listen, listen to the stories ...

The Monster

Long ago, in a time that lives even beyond the old ones' memories, there was a terrible monster called Man Eagle. Cold, dark and evil was his shadow: he stole away beautiful girls and young women, tortured them cruelly for four days, and then ate them alive.

For many years every woman and girl trembled at the mention of Man Eagle's name. They begged their husbands and sons, fathers and brothers to destroy the monster, but none could find a way.

Then one day the evil one dared to seize a young bride called Lakone Mana. Her husband was no ordinary man, but Puukonhoya, one of the Twin Gods of War.

Puukonhoya's grief and anger cracked the sky open like summer lightning. At once he set off upon the monster's trail.

He followed it first to a mountain. This mountain was so steep and tall that its peak was lost far, far up in the Sky. There, in a quiet corner of its lowest slopes, Spider Woman was waiting.

"So you have come," she said. "Watch."

She held a long thread that shimmered in the sunlight. Now she began to weave it with strange magic patterns, shifting, shifting into the shapes of two spirit-girls, dressed in robes of grass.

"Go to the pinyon trees," she told the spirit-girls. "Gather bark, beat it, paint it with resin, then chant over it with spells. Make it look like Man Eagle's rock-strong, impenetrable war-shirt; but make your copy weak and frail, my sisters. Then give it to my grandson who is waiting here. Long before the moon has waxed and waned, your handiwork must bring about the monster's downfall!"

The spirit-girls wandered off and soon the magic shirt was ready. Spider Woman sprinkled it with sacred corn pollen and gave it to Puukonhoya.

Then she turned herself into a tiny spider and scuttled up to hide behind his right ear.

"I will stay here, my grandson. Listen carefully when I whisper and everything will go well. Now look: here is Mole. He is your uncle, and the first thing you must do is follow him."

Mole began to dig. He dug a tunnel straight up, through the dark heart of the mountain. Hidden from Man Eagle's spying eyes, Puukonhoya climbed up after him, right to the top.

The mountain peak was a cold, misty wasteland.

"Be patient," whispered Spider Woman, "the birds are coming."

At that very moment, an eagle flew down, plucked Puukonhoya into his beak and soared with him into the clouds. Up . . . up . . . the eagle tossed him away to a brown hawk. High . . . high . . . the hawk tossed him to a grey hawk – who in turn threw him further, to a red hawk. Far, far beyond the top of the world they travelled!

At last, in a lost corner of the Sky, the fourth bird dropped him gently at the foot of a leaning cliff. Right at the top, in a gleam of ice, stood Man Eagle's house. A long ladder hung down from the door; but its rungs were made from knife blades.

"Grandmother," said Puukonhoya, "tell me what to do."

"Look to your right," whispered the spider. "A sumac bush is growing there. Gather its berries, then look to your left. Lizard will be waiting. Give him the berries: he will chew them into paste, then spit them back to you. Smear the paste onto the rungs to make them blunt and smooth. Then climb!"

Puukonhoya did all these things. Soon he was standing at the doorway to Man Eagle's lair. He went in.

The first room seemed to be empty.

"Look," whispered Spider Woman, "there is Man Eagle's rock-strong, impenetrable war-shirt lying on the floor. Pick it up and put it on, and in its place lay out the spirit-girls' magic copy of the shirt. Be quick!"

He did as she said; and then he passed through to the second room. There he found his weeping bride Lakone Mana, tied up with rough, thick ropes.

"Hurry, hurry!" whispered Spider Woman. "Do not waste time!"

So Puukonhoya threw his beloved a longing kiss, then turned away and went on.

In the third room he found Man Eagle.

The monster was snoring in his sleep; but as soon as he heard footsteps, he awoke with a foul shriek, rushed past Puukonhoya into the first room and put on what he thought was his own rock-strong, impenetrable war-shirt.

"So!" roared the monster. "How dare you come to my house! What do you want of me?"

"I want my wife," said Puukonhoya. "I have come to free Lakone Mana."

"Oh-ho-ho! So that's your game! Do you think I hand out nice tasty women like presents?" Man Eagle's ugly beak was foaming and steaming. "If you want her, my friend, you'll have to gamble for her – with your life! Oh yes, we'll have a contest or two, that's what we'll do. It's a long time since I enjoyed a bit of sport. If you win, I might let you have her; but if *I* win (as I know I will, for I am the greatest, I am unconquerable!) I shall keep the lady and kill you. Agreed?"

"Agreed!" cried Puukonhoya.

"Then come, sit down. We'll start by smoking together."

The monster brought out two enormous pipes, each as big as a man, and filled them with coarse tobacco.

"Do not be fool enough to think that these are pipes of peace," said he. "The tobacco I keep is tainted with poison. You must smoke more of it than I can without passing out, if you want to win this contest."

He lit the pipes at his fire and they both began to puff away.

In Puukonhoya's ear, Spider Woman was whispering,

"Sit still! Your Uncle Mole is beneath you, burrowing a hole."

In this way, as Puukonhoya puffed, the smoke passed straight through his body, out into Mole's tunnel and to the clean air beyond.

So the poison took no hold on him. But Man Eagle breathed it deep into his lungs. At last he grew so dizzy that he could take no more.

"Stop!" he roared. "All right, you have won the first round, but there is much more yet. Come outside!"

On the edge of the cliff were two gigantic antlers, each thicker than a man's body.

"Take this and break it into two halves," commanded Man Eagle. "I shall break the other. Whoever does it first, wins."

While he spoke, Spider Woman flew onto Puukonhoya's antler. She ran round its girth; and where she ran she left a crack, finer than a cobweb, almost invisible but very deep.

"Now!" cried Man Eagle. They both began to strain at the antlers. Sweat sizzled on the monster's brow as he struggled; but Puukonhoya snapped his horn quickly in two, along the crack that Spider Woman had made.

"Yash-yash-yash!" yelled Man Eagle in his fury. "So you think you're stronger than me, do you? Right! You see those trees over there? You take that one, I'll take this, and let us see who is quicker to pull them up by the roots. This time, I shall certainly beat you!"

He strode to the trees and Puukonhoya followed; but Mole, unseen, got there first. In a flash he had gnawed away all the roots from Puukonhoya's tree.

"One, two, three . . . PULL!" shouted the monster, and they both began to heave at the trees. Man Eagle groaned and cursed; but thanks to Mole's quick work, Puukonhoya plucked his from the ground like a flower.

Man Eagle's filthy talons scratched the ground with rage.

"Hai-hai-hai! Well, if you are really such a strong-man you will have an appetite to prove it. Come inside again, friend. You will see, I have a feast all ready just for you."

They went back into his house, where a vast spread of delicious food had miraculously appeared. There were piles of bread, steaming bean soups, great joints of meat, vegetables and every kind of fruit: enough to feed an entire town.

"Eat!" cried Man Eagle. "Eat it all, to the last crumb. If you can do this, you are the winner. But if you leave even the tiniest morsel – then tonight you shall watch me eat your lovely wife for my own dinner!"

In the secret hollows of Puukonhoya's ear, Spider Woman whispered,

"Pass the food down. Uncle Mole is digging for you again."

So Puukonhoya squatted on the floor and pretended to cram the food into his mouth. But really he let it drop into the deep, deep shaft that

Mole had tunnelled out under his feet. The food disappeared down and away, and very soon the whole feast was gone.

Puukonhoya stood up.

"Four times you have challenged me," he said to Man Eagle, "and four times I have won. So! Now I shall fetch Lakone Mana and take her home, as we agreed."

"Wait!" replied the monster. He spread his dark wings across the door to bar the way. "There remains but one last test; and for this your pretty wife herself must help."

He led Puukonhoya into the gloomy chamber where Lakone Mana still waited. Now the War God saw that on either side of her were two towering piles of logs. Flames leaped from Man Eagle's mouth as he lit a brand. Then, untying the ropes which bound Lakone Mana, he thrust the brand into her trembling hand.

"Now," he said. "Your husband will sit on this pile and I will sit on the other. You, my little beauty, will set fire to both. Then you will watch your husband go up in flames – but *I* will emerge from the fire, ravishing hungry and ready to eat you up, for I am the greatest, I am unconquerable!"

With the monster's beak gnashing at her, Lakone Mana had no choice but to obey. The dry wood caught light at once. Man Eagle's vast wings fanned the flames and the fire crackled and roared, burning brightly, white-hot.

Puukonhoya endured it, calm and safe – for he was wearing the monster's war-shirt, rock-hard and impenetrable, coated with cool, wet barbs of ice.

But the shirt that Man Eagle had hurried to put on was the frail copy of bark and resin made by Spider Woman's spirit-girls. The flames engulfed it at once and in a thick, blinding fury of smoke, the evil monster was destroyed!

Puukonhoya saw it. He leaped from the fire and swept his wife into his arms. Hand in hand, they started for the door . . .

"Not so fast!" called a voice.

They turned. Spider Woman, in her true form, stood there glaring at them severely.

"Yes indeed, you have won, my grandson," she said. "But remember

43

this: it is through my help, not by your own strength or cleverness. Swallow your triumph, and learn how to be humble and generous. Now then! Take some of this sacred corn pollen: sprinkle it over the monster's ashes."

Puukonhoya lowered his eyes in shame and dropped Lakone Mana's hand. He did as his grandmother told him. At once the ashes began to sizzle. Strange clouds of smoke grew from them, slowly, slowly, into the shape of a young, handsome man.

"I greet you, Man Eagle," said Spider Woman to the stranger. "Well, well, you have been outwitted at last! Now, after countless terrible seasons, here you are again in the shape to which you were born. Do you wish to keep it? Will you give up your evil ways?"

"Oh Grandmother – yes!" cried the man who had been a monster. "And may all the gods one day forgive me!"

The little old woman made no reply, but gave a curious chuckle. Then, quick as a blink, she turned herself back into a spider and scuttled to her old place behind Puukonhoya's ear.

"Now, everything is complete and you may go," she whispered. "Hurry, hurry, hurry: the four great birds are waiting to carry you down again. Yes, and your dear wife is rightly anxious to be home."

The Boy Who Was Kidnapped by Eagles

There was a boy called Blue Wing who was said to be wild and bad. All day long his mother, his father and his two sisters worked hard together in the fields under the hot sun, but Blue Wing was never with them.

Instead, he spent all his time roaming the mountains, catching eagles which he cared for in magnificent cages.

The priests were grateful to him, for they needed eagles for their sacred ceremonies. But Blue Wing's family accused him of laziness and of wasting the days.

"Your muscles are as strong as our father's," complained his sisters, "yet you leave all the ploughing and hoeing and carrying water to us. The holy men have time enough to see to their eagles themselves: leave them, and do the work you were born to do!"

At last the two girls grew so exhausted and angry that they decided to take revenge. One day, while he was out, they crept into the eagles' cage and beat the sacred birds with their brooms until their beautiful feathers were all scattered. Then, leaving the cage doors open so that the birds could fly to freedom, they hurried away.

Soon Blue Wing returned. His heart froze with the dread of evil omens when he saw the eagles were gone, and their plumage scattered to the winds.

But as he stood there staring, the eagles suddenly appeared above him, calling down the sorry tale of what his sisters had done.

"Because of this we are leaving your village for ever," they said. "Boy – you must come with us!"

Blue Wing looked up at the huge, wheeling birds and now his heart soared. They had chosen him, of all people, to fly with them! Perhaps they would take him to meet the gods. He raised his arms and the eagles swooped down to carry him off to the Sky.

Far, far he flew with them, riding on their great strong backs. The sun moved round and sank in a blaze of crimson flames. In the quiet darkness, now they rose up through a hole in the clouds.

At last, high in the Sky world, they stopped on a bleak, lonely crag.

"Stay here!" the eagles told him. "Wait, alone. Search the darkest corners of your heart. Then you may understand why we are punishing you for your sisters' cruelty. If such wisdom ever comes, then at last you may be free."

For the second time, Blue Wing's heart froze.

"But I am your friend!" he cried. "I have always served you. It is my sisters who deserve punishment. I should . . ."

His words fell like ash into the silence, for the eagles were gone.

It was dark and lonely, empty, cold. He was humbled and afraid.

But by and by, out of the darkness, a wren appeared.

"Help!" called Blue Wing hoarsely.

The wren stared at him for a moment with her beady eye; then flew away.

Soon she came back, and this time a spider was riding on her back. The spider spoke, and her voice was like an old, old woman's.

"Do not think you are friendless, for I will help you."

She waved her eight legs and spun a dazzling thread into the shape of two enormous turkey feathers.

"Sleep between these tonight: they will keep you warm."

Then both spider and wren disappeared and the darkness was complete.

Blue Wing lay upon one feather and placed the other on top of him. All through the freezing night he dreamed that he was sleeping in a soft, warm bed.

He woke when it was light and saw the wren again, waiting. She led him across the rocks to a dark, narrow crevice.

"Pluck the feathers from my back," she said.

In wonder, Blue Wing did it. One by one, the wren took the feathers in her beak and, flying into the crevice, poked them neatly into the rock. Now they formed the rungs of a long, long ladder.

"Climb down to the ground," she said.

Blue Wing did so. As soon as he was there, the wren fluttered back up the ladder and returned the feathers to her body.

"The spider's hole is close at hand," she called down to him. "Go and find her." Then she flew away.

Blue Wing looked carefully about. Soon he spied a large hole, its entrance masked by silvery cobwebs. A little old grey woman with piercing eyes was resting beside it.

"You are welcome," said she, in the same voice that he had heard last night. "I am Grandmother Spider. Come into my *kiva*. Stay a while with me."

So Blue Wing followed her down, down into the dark underground chamber where Spider Woman dwelt. She fed him well, and let him sleep.

The next morning, Blue Wing climbed out and went exploring. Soon he came to a lake with many game birds drinking water from the shore. He stoned one and carried it back to the *kiva*. There he shared the good meat with Spider Woman – and was rewarded with her praise.

"It is good to have a young man to hunt for me," she said. "Perhaps your family has lost a better son than they ever knew. You may stay here for as long as you wish, if you will keep my larder full with meat. I will let you enjoy your freedom. But listen carefully: you must never follow the path that leads towards the sunset, for one lives there who is cunning, dangerous and evil."

Now Blue Wing was happy. How proud he was to bring food to the Grandmother of all Earth! Every night they ate together in the warmth of her *kiva*, and Blue Wing listened quietly to her stories.

Yet wildness still stirred his heart and he was curious. Often and often he puzzled over her warning to avoid the sunset path.

"I am not afraid, for I have flown with the eagles," he thought. "Who knows, perhaps if I find this evil one, I may even be able to destroy him. Surely that would make Spider Woman glad."

So one morning, in secret, he set out across the Sky desert towards the West.

He walked a long way: he saw nothing and met no-one. But at last he came to another *kiva*.

A man was sitting beside the entrance. He was very wrinkled, very ugly. His hooded eyelids were so long that they hung right down over his chest.

Blue Wing stopped uncertainly, waiting. Slowly, slowly the wrinkled one pushed his eyelids back and peered at him.

"Ah," said he, "a visitor! The world has grown old since the last time anyone came to see me. Well, well, well! I am pleased to know you boy. Come – come down into my *kiva*. There we shall play some gambling games together."

Blue Wing felt pity for this hideous old man who seemed so utterly alone. Forgetting Spider Woman's warnings, he readily agreed.

For many hours they played games of chance together; and each game ended with Blue Wing as the loser.

At last and of a sudden, Hooded Lid called a stop.

"Ho boy! I have beaten you countless times. Settle your debts! What will you give me in payment for your losses?"

Blue Wing held out his empty hands.

"I have nothing to pay you with," he said, "and I am far from home. But think: I have given you hours of company and friendship, and for this I beg you to have mercy."

Hooded Lid's dry, thin lips curled into an ugly snarl.

"Cheat!" he shrieked. "You agreed to gamble, yet you knew full well you could not pay me. No, I shall not be merciful!"

Then he pounced upon Blue Wing, seized him in a strong grip, and tied him up so tightly that he could not move. He pushed him out through the *kiva* entrance and made him lie outside, wedged there like a door to keep out the cold.

Blue Wing was helpless. Night dropped onto the empty desert: indeed, it was cold, very cold. Wretchedly he lay there, cursing himself for his foolishness.

Then – suddenly – Spider Woman was beside him.

"Oh, tut-tut, tut-tut, when will you ever learn to listen to good advice?" she whispered.

Just as last time, she conjured up two magic turkey feathers to keep him warm.

"Now you must wait through the long night," she said. "But have no

48

fear: I shall be back."

Early in the morning she returned, and Mole was with her. They pulled Blue Wing away from the entrance, but they could not untie him, for his ropes were knotted with magic.

So Spider Woman called down into the *kiva*.

"I greet you Hooded Lid! I hear you are fond of games. Come out into the sunlight then, and let us see who is the better player."

The evil one climbed out at once, rubbing his wrinkled hands together at the thought of another day's gambling.

Spider Woman set out her gaming cups and challenged Hooded Lid to guess under which one she had hidden the ball. While he considered, Mole was busy: he dug fast and deep underground and hid the ball in his tunnels. Thus whichever way the evil one guessed, it was impossible for him to win.

He played and lost, played and lost, over and over.

"I am the winner every time!" declared Spider Woman at last. "They say that you like your debts to be settled quickly, Hooded Lid. So: pay me at once with this boy."

"Not so fast, Grandmother," replied the evil one, blinking secretly behind his long eyelids. "This boy owes me much more than I owe you. If you want him, first you must perform a service for me.

"Look, over there stands a kwingwi bush. Its roots are so long that they hang down into my *kiva* like snakes: every night they give me nightmares. They are so tough that for a hundred winters I have tried and failed to pull the bush up. If you can do this for me – then, though it pains me, I swear I will give you back this wretch of a boy."

As he spoke, Mole slipped away and dug a new tunnel, under the kwingwi bush. He gnawed at its roots until nothing was left of them.

Then Spider Woman began to pull. At once the bush came easily out of the ground.

Now Hooded Lid was awed and humbled. He muttered Spider Woman's praises and, without further ado, released Blue Wing from his bindings. Then, begging them to wait, he hurried into his *kiva*. When he reappeared from the darkness he was hauling after him a great sack of treasure.

"Grandmother, take these," he said. "Once they belonged to other lost travellers; I confess I killed and ate them! I ask you to scatter their things back to Earth. If their families find them, perhaps it may help their spirits to rest in peace."

Spider Woman took the treasures and Hooded Lid backed away from her like a frightened fly.

She led Blue Wing away.

"You have seen many things," she said. "I hope this has helped you to grow wiser."

They went along a trail until they came to a place where the clouds opened to a hole beneath their feet.

"This is the door through which the eagles brought you to the Sky," she said. "It is time for you to go home."

She spun a long, long thread and dropped it through the hole: "Climb down it."

Thus Blue Wing passed through the clouds and the clear air until at last he was standing again on the Earth.

Slowly, a little afraid, he walked home. His father, his mother, his two sisters were all amazed to see him.

"Marvellous things have happened to me," he told them. "I am changed. Now I wish only to work with you and for you."

When they heard these words, they were glad.

She Is
Everywhere

Come now, we will just sweep the house out, then we will take time to talk . . .

No, no, don't sweep that corner! Can't you see the spider there, the little grey one? Look how quiet and grave she sits, steadily, steadily spinning . . .

Yes, that is Grandmother Spider. Take care, keep your broom well away from her, be careful not to break her web.

You know, she is watching us. Here in the cool darkness of the house there is little to fear; but out in the bright sunlight, ah . . . Listen, I will tell you what happened once to a stranger, a traveller from distant lands who did not know.

My brothers saw him passing as they were working their fields in the valley. They called out a greeting: he told them he would climb up, up to our village here on top of the steep, rocky *mesa*. You know well that there are two paths: he chose the steeper one, because it also looks to be the shorter way. My brothers warned him strongly against it, urging him to take the longer route, but he laughed and would not listen.

Half way up this steep path, a spring gushes out. Beside the water, Grandmother Spider often sits in her true form, a little grey woman, as old as she is beautiful.

The stranger never reached our village. He set off up that path, but he was never seen again . . .

Everyone knows what happened to him.

He came to the spring. Spider Woman smiled at him. He stopped and spoke with her.

Oh, soft but strong, strong and tight is her web!

No sooner had he spoken, than Spider Woman began to call him.

They say her summons is so sweet and dark, rich with promised secrets. She beckoned; yet still he hesitated. Then in the sharp white sunlight he saw the shadows of her two grandsons, the Twin Gods of War.

"Go with her, follow her!" That was the voice of Younger Brother, smilingly urging him on.

"No! Stop! Go back!" That was Older Brother hissing his warning. "If you follow her now, you will never return!"

But the stranger had walked where only the initiated should go, and it was too late. He could not stop, he could not go back. Spider Woman held him with her silken thread. Down, down, she led him, into the rock, into the black womb darkness of our mother, the Earth, where all living creatures must begin and end.

I tell you this, that you may understand why we love and fear and respect her.

For she is goodness, but she is also death. And she is everywhere in the corners of our houses, waiting and watching, watching and waiting.

PART 3

OLD MAN
COYOTE
AND HIS
TRICKS

Why Coyote
Looks So Dirty

Listen, and I'll tell you about Coyote.

He claims to walk with the gods: oh, he can boast all right! "Who put the sun in the Sky?" he says. "Who taught you to grow corn? Who made the world such a fine place to live in? It was me, me, me!"

Yes, he's clever – and cunning too. But just remember this: all along, Old Man Coyote is no more than a mangy wild dog. And his fur's filthy – the colour of dust.

And yet, they say that once he was beautiful bright green, like the grass and leaves and all things that grow. But Coyote, he wasn't satisfied. He wanted to be blue, the colour of the Sky.

So he went on the prowl, looking for someone who could tell him how to change colour. But everyone knew what he was like, ohoh, and no-one was willing to help him.

At last he stopped asking and started spying. And he kept his eye fixed right on Bluebird, because he was just the shade that Coyote wanted to be. So he followed Bluebird and followed him, until they came to a secret lake with water bluer even than the Sky.

As soon as he got there, Bluebird jumped into the water with a splash. He took a quick swim; then out he came again. Once, twice, three times, four times he splashed in and out of the Sky-reflecting water; and then he flew away. By this time, his feathers were looking brighter and bluer than ever.

"Hey, that's easy!" chortled Coyote. He copied everything he'd seen Bluebird doing. One, two, three, four times he took a splash and a swim in the magic lake.

And when he came out, sure enough, he was looking as blue as blue! Then he felt wonderful, really proud of himself. He went running home as fast as he could, and all the time he was looking around, right and left, here and there, to make sure that the other animals were all admiring him. He even kept twisting his head to look right behind, because he wanted to see if his shadow were blue too.

Well, he was so busy showing off that he didn't notice where he was going:

Crash!

. . . straight into a tree! He hit it with such a thump that he went sprawling onto the ground. And the ground was dirty, all churned up with thick, wet mud.

Deep in the mud, Coyote went rolling about and writhing, trying to get off his back and onto his legs. I can tell you this: it took him a long, long time.

At last he got himself the right way up again. But just look, the mud was stuck and matted deep, deep in his fur. It was so bad that no-one could possibly see the beautiful blue underneath.

And that's how it happened. That's why, ever since that day and every day, Old Man Coyote has looked as dull and horrible as dirt.

How Coyote
Got His Tail

Long ago, none of the birds had any feathers. However, there was one exception: a huge and terrible eagle who lived alone right on top of a mountain. The other birds were all very jealous of him. At last, a great flock of them flew in from the four corners of the Earth, determined to seize his feathers for themselves.

First they went up the mountain to beg him to share them out peacefully; but the eagle was vain and selfish, and he refused. So the birds agreed that the only way to get what they longed for was to kill him.

They got out their bows and arrows; they began to shoot. And right in the middle of it all, who should come along but Coyote. Of course, he joined in: if something wild was happening, that old man didn't want to miss out!

By the time the eagle was finally slain, it was nightfall. Everyone was worn out – especially Coyote. So they agreed to leave the body just where it was until the morning. Then, as soon as the sun was out, they would all go up the mountain and have a share-out of the feathers.

Well, it seemed that whoever got up the peak first, he was going to have the first pick of the finest feathers for himself. Old Man Coyote couldn't stop brooding about this. He was really worried that he'd miss out on the best.

He said to himself: "I've got to be the first one up tomorrow and there's only one way to make sure of it: I'll have to keep myself awake all night."

You know Coyote, he's always full of tricks. Off he went, scratching around, until he found himself two little sticks. He sharpened them at both ends. Then he propped them up, one in each eye, to keep his eyelids open.

But he was so tired that he fell asleep anyway. He started to snore, and his eyelids began to press themselves together, despite the sharpened sticks. Very soon the sticks had pierced right the way through the skin. So instead of propping his eyes wide open, now they pinned them tightly shut!

When Coyote finally awoke, the sun was already high in the sky. But he didn't know that, because he couldn't see. Oh, when he found that his trick had gone bad on him, I can tell you, he was roaring with rage!

Soon all the birds came down from the mountain top, resplendent in their bright new feathers. The first thing they saw was poor Old Man Coyote hopping around, trying to get the sticks out of his eyes. They just laughed and laughed!

But after a while, they took pity and decided to help him. They pulled out the sticks with their beaks, and then Coyote could see everything. And of course the first thing *he* saw was that all the feathers, every last one, had been taken.

That made him hopping angry again.

"Hey, hey what's the matter Coyote?" everyone shouted. "You'd look stupid with feathers stuck all over you anyway – you're no bird!"

Coyote, he just growled and bared his teeth at them. He couldn't bear to think he was the only one going home with nothing.

But he was wrong: the birds had kept a share for him after all.

"The eagle had this thing hanging from his backside," they said. "None of us wanted it, but we thought it might look fine and handsome on you."

And they gave him a tail. It was long and droopy, like a thick piece of rotten old brushwood.

Coyote snatched it and stuck it on. He couldn't see it back there; but he could feel it sweeping the ground as he ran along, he could see the trail it dragged through the dust.

Then he was proud: no-one else had anything like it!

He's worn it ever since.

Why Coyote
Howls at the Sky

The world was young; and it was night time.

Black, black was the night. It swallowed everything up in its darkness. You could see nothing; if you wanted to travel, it was impossible to find the way.

There were many creatures who longed for the night to be a friend to them. If only the black Sky would shine with light – then they could hunt and eat, travel and play; ah, then they would truly be happy.

So they called upon He-Who-Made-the-World to help.

He-Who-Made-the-World heard and was with them. He walked along a river and found a stone. The stone sparkled and shone like the bright flames of a fire. He-Who-Made-the-World threw it up, up, up.

The stone lodged in the Sky: it shone with brilliant light!

He-Who-Made-the-World said: "This is the first star. It will stay in this place for ever. If you are travelling and lose your way, look for it: use it to find your path home.

"But this work is not yet finished. There must be more stars, many, many to lighten the night. They will move round and round this home-star for ever. And you, the animals, shall make them.

"Go to the river. Find stones like I found. Gather them in your paws and claws, in your beaks and mouths. Throw them carefully into the Sky, so that they form pictures of yourselves."

So the animals and birds did as the creator had told them. Soon, high above them, many star pictures hung: the constellations.

But some creatures are small and weak. They could not gather enough stones, they could not throw them as far as the Sky.

So He-Who-Made-the-World called upon Coyote:

"Hey trickster! Here is a whole sack full of the shining stones. Take them. Use them to help the small ones, the weak ones to make their portraits."

Coyote peered into the huge, heavy sack and growled with anger. It would take him many, many nights to toss up all these stones into neat little pictures. He would never have the patience.

So he opened the sack wide. With a single, careless throw, he hurled its entire contents into the sky.

Then the darkness was lit by a mad, swirling star-storm.

Up and down, round through the night the stars swarmed and circled. But at last, like all things, they grew quiet and still and fixed themselves into patterns.

Into patterns – but not pictures.

That is why, even today, many of the constellations seem vague to us, unfinished.

Now Coyote gazed up at the stars and laughed aloud at the turmoil he had made.

But his laughter quickly turned to fury. For he had been so eager to get rid of all the star stones that he had forgotten to make a picture of himself!

Since that distant time, whenever night falls Coyote howls at the Sky. Ah, imagine his anguish: amongst a thousand brilliant constellations he – the great trickster – will never shine!

How Coyote
Made Winter

You know Coyote: he thinks he's a god. Yet whenever he gets mixed up in something, it always goes wrong.

There was a time when he couldn't even hunt for himself, couldn't catch anything. Soon he was starving. Then he started to trail around after Eagle.

Eagle, he's a brilliant hunter, he always catches more than he can eat. So each day, after he had eaten his fill, he left what was over for Coyote. Of course, that suited Coyote really well.

But Eagle felt that Coyote was being lazy, taking advantage.

"Go and catch your own food," he said.

"Oooh-ooh," whined Coyote. "I can't catch anything because it's too dark to see properly."

In those days, you know, the sun and the moon did not hang in the Sky. They were kept in a secret box by the people of a little village, a long way off in the West. These people only let out a tiny, tiny speck of light at a time. So day or night, it was always murky twilight.

"Then we will go to the people who guard the sun and the moon," said Eagle. "If we can persuade them to make more light, you can hunt for yourself and not pester me any more."

Coyote agreed. So they travelled westward until at last they came to the Village of Light.

The people of the village were watching a festival, with dancers dressed as *kachina* spirits. As they danced, they carried a big, beautifully decorated box. From time to time they opened it, and then golden sunlight and silver moonlight spilled out.

"There's the light," whispered Eagle. "We must ask if we can have some."

Coyote shook his head. "They are bound to say 'no'," he hissed, "or else they won't let us have enough. We must *steal* the whole box for ourselves!"

Eagle hesitated. But because he was so anxious to get rid of Coyote, eventually he agreed.

When the ceremony was over, all the villagers went back to their houses to sleep. The *kachina* dancers stowed the sacred box carefully away in a deep underground *kiva*, and then they too went home.

As soon as everything was quiet, Eagle dropped down into the *kiva*. He seized the sacred box in his talons, and then he flew away home.

He went so fast that Coyote, bounding along behind, could scarcely keep up.

"Hey Eagle," he shouted, "let me see the box!"

"No, no," Eagle called back, "you'll drop it or break it. Whatever you try to do always goes wrong."

"*Please* Eagle!"

"No."

"Eagle, just one quick peep . . ."

"No, no, no!"

"Eagle – let me see the box!"

That was the fourth time Coyote had asked him, and the power of four cannot be refused. So now Eagle had to give in.

Reluctantly he flew to the ground and passed the box to Coyote.

"I entrust it to your keeping," he said. "But friend: you must promise not to open it."

"I promise," said Coyote; but his eyes were sly.

Soon Eagle had flown far ahead again.

"He is hiding something from me," said Coyote to himself. "Why should I do as he says?"

Then he flung the lid open wide.

At once, the moon flew out on silvery wings and soared away, away, away. And after it, out came the sun, a dazzling golden fireball, spinning and speeding far, far up to the Sky.

As the moon and the sun went, all the light, every last drop, disappeared from the Earth. And all the warmth went too.

So it was very cold, very dark. The flowers and leaves and crops shrivelled up and died, the lakes froze and it began to snow.

That was the first winter. Coyote made it with his mischief. Since then it has returned every year to mock him.

Huh! If it wasn't for that old man's meddling, we could have enjoyed summer all the time.

Coyote
and the Acorns

Coyote, he's really fond of food; but he's got no idea about cooking. They say he never even tried to cook for himself – until the day he tasted sour acorns.

"Mmmm!"

Coyote thought they were so delicious, he begged his friends to feed him more, more, MORE!

At last they got tired of his greed. "Go and cook some yourself!" they told him.

Then Coyote began to whine and whimper,

"That's not fair! You know I can't cook."

"There's nothing clever about making sour acorns," they replied. "All you do is collect some raw acorns together in a pot, pour water over them and press the whole lot down with a heavy weight. Leave them for two days, then take a look and a sniff: they'll be just ready to eat."

Coyote snarled, "Stop mocking me. I know cooking's much more difficult than that. Tell me the *real* way to make them!"

"But we've told you. You, you're not just greedy, you're an idiot too!"

"Ow-ow-ow!" Coyote howled like a baby. "Tell me, tell me, tell me!"

Then the other animals began to nudge each other, and the look in their eyes said, *it's our turn to play a trick on this old man who's always tricking us.*

"All right," they said. "There *is* more to it than we made out. This is what you really do. You get a canoe, put it on the river, and fill it right up to the top with acorns. Then you tip it upside down, so that the acorns all fall into the water. You need to leave them there for a good, long soaking; then you go along the river bank and pick them out again. After that, they're all ready to eat."

At this Coyote was satisfied – really pleased. He went galloping home to tell his grandmother.

"Hey Grandma, you know all those acorns you went out collecting when the moon was new? I've just learned the most delicious way to cook them."

"You leave them alone!" screeched the old lady. She knew Coyote and his ways well, too well. But Coyote was never one to listen to advice, not even from an elder.

As soon as he was sure she wasn't looking, he sneaked to his grandmother's storage pot and carried it on his back down to the river. He tipped all the acorns out of the pot into a canoe; then out of the canoe into the water.

Then he rubbed his paws together and licked his chops.

"Just cooking nicely," said he.

It wasn't long before his grandmother came hobbling after him in a frenzy of rage.

"Coyote, you get back those acorns of mine at once!"

"As soon as they're ready, I'll fish them out Grandma, don't you worry. Just wait until you taste them!"

After a while, he started off along the bank. All the time, he was looking for the acorns to come floating in. "They'll be nicely cooked and soured by now," he thought.

Poor Old Man Coyote, he never learns. Those acorns – every single one of them – stayed just where he'd thrown them, down, down among the stones and mud, deep at the bottom of the river.

It wasn't long before he realised he'd been tricked. Then he was mad, then he was hungry! "*Ow-ow-ooow!*" You could hear him howling right beyond the other side of the mountains.

He went wheedling back to his grandmother, but she wouldn't feed him. Oh, oh, but he could smell something good, wonderfully good bubbling away in her pot.

"It's nothing but dung," the old lady told him. "That's all we've got since you threw away my acorns."

Coyote knew he was being mocked again. He was so ashamed, he slunk away, he went to roll in the dirt.

PART 4

STRANGE JOURNEYS, MARVELLOUS HAPPENINGS

The Great
Mystery Lake

There was once a boy called Long Arrow whose mother and father were both dead. No-one wanted to adopt him, so he lived like a wild creature on the edge of the camp, fighting with the dogs over scraps of food, sleeping in rough hollows under the stars.

But for many moons he was watched by a chief called Good Running. This man and his wife had no children: their hearts were big and lonely. At last they took the boy in and gave him good food and plenty of kindness.

Long Arrow grew in their warmth like a flower under the summer sun. He was quick to learn and soon became skilled in everything a young brave should be able to do.

Yet though he grew steadily cleverer and stronger, everyone seemed to scorn him. The girls laughed in his face when he tried to court them; and the other young men called him a ragamuffin and a fool.

So he went to Good Running and said,

"Father, my heart will be heavy until I can prove myself to be a better man than those who mock me. Tell me what I must do."

Good Running stood thoughtfully, hooding his eyes against the sun.

"There is a lake far, far away," he said. "Many young men have tried to find it, but no-one who has begun the search has ever returned. At the bottom of this lake it is said that some strange spirit-people dwell. Everyone who speaks of them is afraid. These spirit-people are said to share their world-below-water with animals more beautiful and powerful than any on Earth. They are as large as elks. Their bodies are like music, shaped to run in harmony with the wind. They are strong and gentle and clever. They can do all the work that a dog can do, and much more. All who know of them long to find them. No-one has ever done so."

"I will go to this lake," said Long Arrow at once. "I will bring back some of these wonderful animals."

Good Running smiled and nodded.

"Then go to the medicine men, my son, and ask them for the secrets that will make you into a man, in preparation for your journey."

So Long Arrow went to the holy ones. They purified him in the steam of the sweat-lodge and taught him how to smoke the sacred pipe of peace. They gave him a medicine-bag of magic herbs and a shield painted with patterns to ward off danger. Above all, they taught him the whispered knowledge of the Great Mystery, and how to keep courage and generosity in the depths of his heart.

When he was ready, Long Arrow set off.

He walked southwards for four days until he came to a small, stagnant pond. On its banks sat a stranger, all shrivelled and pinched and scraggy, giving off a foul, watery stench with every breath he drew.

Long Arrow remembered that he too had once been poor and wretched. He greeted the foul one courteously and offered him some food from his bundle.

The stranger snatched it with an unpleasant cackle.

"Ahah, I've been waiting for you!" he cried. "You're looking for the Great Mystery Lake aren't you? Well, don't think you're anywhere near it yet. But listen, you've been polite so I'll tell you this: you'll have to keep on walking for four-times-four days, until you come to another stretch of water. It's bigger than this, and my uncle who lives there is bigger than I am too; but you won't like him any more than you like me, oh no! If you're lucky he'll talk to you, if you're not, he won't. Now, I don't want you here any more – be off with you, grrr! get on your way!"

Long Arrow thanked him; then, with a sigh, he went on with his journey. For sixteen more days he followed the trail of the noon-day sun, climbing high into some wooded hills, until at last he came to a small lake.

As he stood staring at the shimmering water, the ground began to shudder and quake. Suddenly, there before him stood a huge, gnarled giant clutching a blood-red flint spear in his fist.

Long Arrow swallowed his weariness to give a greeting; then he offered the giant a morsel of dried meat, apologising that by now his bundle was almost empty.

"Oh, ho, ho!" roared the giant. His voice echoed and sparked like a thunder storm between the craggy rocks. "Aren't you afraid of me?"

"No," said Long Arrow. "The only thing I fear is my own failure."

The giant gave a rumble of laughter.

"Ah, so you are the one I've been expecting! Well, well, well, my lad, know this: you've got a long way to go yet! Just keep walking southward for another four-times-four days. If your legs haven't crumbled to dust by then, and your belly hasn't shrivelled up with hunger, you'll see the Great Mystery Lake . . . and thereabouts you might just come across my grandfather." He roared again with laughter. "Ah-hah-hah! But the chances are – by the time you get there, he'll be nowhere to be seen!"

Then he gave Long Arrow a stinging slap across the shoulders and vanished into the water.

So Long Arrow stumbled on once more, counting the days. On the last evening he climbed high into some mountains and found himself on the shores of the vastest lake he had ever seen.

It was dark, deep and silent, framed by towering snow-capped peaks and glittering waterfalls of ice. No bird disturbed its stillness. No fish rippled its surface. Nothing moved under the blue sky that melted into its waters.

Long Arrow was exhausted and almost dead with hunger. He sank down and at once fell into a long, deep sleep.

When he woke, the sun was high. A young boy was crouching by his side, dressed in a soft white buckskin robe, decorated with porcupine quills of many rainbow colours.

"Come," he said softly, "my grandfather does not like to be kept waiting."

With these words the boy rose and, in a flash of brilliant blue, turned himself into a kingfisher. Then he dived straight down into the lake.

Long Arrow stared after him. He imagined death by drowning; he pictured what slow, cruel tortures the underwater spirit-people might weave about him with their spells.

But he shook himself like a dog, took a deep breath and plunged in after the kingfisher.

Down, down, down he sank. His eyes were open – and the waters parted before him.

At last he came to the bottom. He stood on dry, white sand that sloped gently down, still further, to a circular valley. Alone in the middle stood a tipi, its walls painted with curious, dazzling patterns.

The kingfisher was perched on top of its poles. As Long Arrow approached, suddenly he changed back into a boy and beckoned,

"Welcome, welcome! Come into my grandfather's house!"

He lifted the door flap and Long Arrow entered. Inside, the tipi was brilliant with treasures: precious stones and exquisite weavings, finely worked shields, weapons and robes.

An old, old man in a floor-length robe sat in their midst. His white hair hung about his shoulders. His black eyes were as fathomless as the Great Mystery Lake itself. He sat very still, waiting and watching, and his deep stillness seemed to flow out into the tipi like soft, seeping water.

Long Arrow trembled in his presence; yet slowly, slowly he forced himself to lift his head and meet those deep, dark eyes.

And the Old One smiled at him.

"Welcome, my grandson. Sit. Eat. Smoke the peace pipe with me. Then we will talk."

A graceful old woman came in, bringing bowls of food: rich, fresh killed meat, juicy berries, steaming hot corn-bread. When Long Arrow had eaten his fill, the Old One filled his pipe with sweet tobacco and they sat quietly together, watching the coiling white smoke carry their prayers to the Sky.

At last the Old One spoke.

"So! You were not afraid to walk into eternity or to dive into the bottomless waters. You were not too proud to share your food with the foul spirits who lurked along the path to taunt you. It is good. Now let me show you what you have travelled all this way to see."

He stood up, leading the way out and up the white shifting sand.

At the top they came to a pasture. And there at last, Long Arrow beheld the wonderful creatures that so long had filled his dreams.

Their bodies shone like polished wood. Their long tails and manes streamed in the breeze like glossy maidens' hair. As he stood there, they turned to meet his gaze with eyes that were at once fiery, gentle and wild.

"These are horses," said the Old One. He whistled and the kingfisher alighted at their feet. "Show him what they can do."

Kingfisher-Boy turned himself again into human shape and jumped upon a horse's back. He galloped round the pasture, then signalled Long Arrow to follow suit.

So Long Arrow too mounted a horse. At once he gave a whoop of sheer delight, for as it ran, he seemed to be soaring through the air like a bird.

Afterwards, the Old One told him:

"I know what is your heart's desire, my grandson. But I shall give you nothing until you can pass this test: tell me – *who am I?*"

Then Long Arrow had no choice but to stay and wait in the world-below-water. He ate well and rested, and often they let him glimpse the horses; yet his whole being ached to solve the Old One's riddle.

Many, many days had passed, and Long Arrow was growing weary with despair. The Old One stood over him, silently shaking his head. Then he turned to go out of the tipi. For an instant the bottom of his long black robe caught against a corner of the door flap and Long Arrow had a fleeting glimpse of his feet . . .

Horse hooves!

"*Grandfather!*" Long Arrow's voice shook and his heart pounded. The old man turned to him, and for only the second time he dared look straight into those deep, brooding eyes.

"I know you! Grandfather, you are . . . the Spirit of the Horses!"

A smile flickered across the Old One's face and he bowed his head in acknowledgement.

"You have been brave and steadfast and patient," he said. "You have watched well and been quick to understand. So – you have passed the test. Now you may ask what you want of me."

"I long for some horses, Grandfather. And I beg you to grant me a safe journey home with them, so that my people may see where I have been and what I have found."

The Old One nodded.

"You shall have half my herd of horses and more, my grandson. Take also this rainbow-quilled belt: it has horse-magic in it. Listen to it closely when the night is quiet, and you will hear the Horse Dance Song: you must learn it carefully and teach it to your people. I shall also give you this long lasso, woven from the hair of a rare white buffalo bull: use it carefully, and it will always bring to you whichever horse you want."

Long Arrow fell to his knees to thank him, but the Old One urged him to rise.

"No, no! Now you must go. Go alone. Walk towards the North for four days. Do not look back. Wear the magic belt I have given you, and carry the lasso. On the fourth day, the horses will come up fast behind you. Catch one with the lasso and ride it home."

Even before this speech was finished, the old woman was bringing Long Arrow bundles of food for his journey, and Kingfisher-Boy was beckoning him to follow him back up through the icy waters of the Great Mystery Lake.

Then he was alone on the empty shore. He turned to the North and began to walk, just as the Old One had told him.

And everything came about as he had been promised.

When at last he rode back into the camp, leading a great herd of the beautiful spirit creatures behind him, all the people were afraid. But after they had heard his story and seen what the horses could do for them, they began to sing Long Arrow's praises.

So it was that the first horses came to the People. Now they could travel swiftly, carry heavy burdens and hunt the buffalo much better: their lives were changed for ever.

The Great
Rabbit Chase

Who would dare to challenge Great Rabbit? Not you, not I, not anyone –
for Great Rabbit can shake the world with his magic!

Yet the trickster is not immune. Wildcat had no fear of him. Wildcat
was fierce, Wildcat had a temper. And rabbit was his favourite food!

One day, Wildcat was starving.

"I'm all shrivelled up," he said. "I need something fat and fine to fill me
up. That Great Rabbit would be just the thing. I'm going to catch and kill
and eat him!"

But Great Rabbit knows everyone's secret thoughts. When he saw
what Wildcat was planning, he laughed out loud. Then he began to leap
away as fast as he could; and every leap he took was as far as a man can
walk in a day.

"*Aaach!*" Wildcat was angry. But he too had magic powers. With a
hiss and a spit he set off on Great Rabbit's trail.

So Great Rabbit leaped and laughed, far, far, far. But he knew that
Wildcat was following him and getting closer; night was falling and the
trickster was getting tired.

Great Rabbit stopped and looked around. He was in the middle of a
vast, snow-covered plain. There was nothing there except for a single tree.

Great Rabbit touched the tree. *Fizzz!* He turned it into a tipi. It was big
and fine, with a fire blazing inside. Great Rabbit sat down and waited for
Wildcat to arrive.

By the time Wildcat got there, it was black-dark and icy cold. He lifted
the door flap and peered in. By the firelight he saw an old chief, sitting
there solemn and still.

Oh Wildcat, what a fool! He didn't see that the chief had two long ears
sticking up on top of his head.

"Greetings, Grandfather," called Wildcat respectfully. "I am looking for a rabbit."

The long-eared chief's eyes flashed but his answer sounded kind:

"Rabbits – they are everywhere; yet to catch them needs much wisdom and strength. Friend, you are welcome to stay here until morning. Then you can continue your rabbit chase renewed and refreshed."

So Wildcat went in and sat down. He ate the bowl of stew that the chief offered him; then he curled up by the fire and went to sleep.

But when he woke in the morning, the tipi and the fire and the long-eared chief were all gone. Instead he found himself lying under a lonely tree, half buried under a snowdrift. His fur and his whiskers were tipped with icicles and his belly was crying with hunger.

"*Aisshh!*" hissed Wildcat. "That Great Rabbit is a fiend and a master of illusion. Just wait till I get my teeth into him: I shall tear him apart, slowly and painfully, limb by limb."

So Wildcat set off on Great Rabbit's trail again. Great Rabbit had made an early start and his leaps were longer than ever; but Wildcat had sworn to catch up with him, driven on and on by his hunger.

That evening, Great Rabbit stopped to rest in the middle of a forest. He trampled down a clearing and scattered huge pine branches all around. *Whissh!* He transformed them into an enormous wigwam. Then the pine-needles began to chatter and laugh, taking the shape of many people making merry as they feasted.

Soon Wildcat arrived. He opened the door and walked in, his eyes popping, his mouth dribbling at the sight of such a spread of delicious food. Two beautiful girls took hold of his paws, one on each side, and led him along to greet the chief.

The chief sat on a high seat. He looked as if he had been expecting Wildcat. But that simpleton was too busy licking his chops to notice that his host had a pair of long white feathers sticking up, one on each side of his head!

The chief invited Wildcat to join the throng and to eat. What a marvellous spread it was: roast meats of every kind, tender baked fish, wild honey, sweet scarlet and purple berries. By the time he had finished, Wildcat felt ready to burst.

Now, one by one, the feasters took turns to stand up and sing a song.

Some told of their heroic deeds in war, others of their skill as hunters; some sang sweet songs of love. Wildcat sat back and dozed, lulled by the music.

But suddenly the white feathered chief pointed at him.

"My friend, we have given you plenty of good food and fine company. In return you must take your turn to honour us with a song."

Wildcat stood up nervously: he had over-eaten and his head was swimming. He opened his mouth and spouted forth the first words that came into his head:

"*I hate rabbits*
But I like their meat;
I love to scalp rabbits
Then have them to eat ..."

The chief held up one hand as a signal for him to stop.

"Friend, your song is truly remarkable. It deserves a special reward."

Wildcat glowed with pleasure.

Then *zonkk!* the chief was hitting him over the head with a tomahawk! *Zonkk, zonkk, zonkk!*

The lodge spun round and faded into nothingness: the food, the warmth, the merrymaking were all gone. Wildcat found himself sprawled out under a canopy of dark, silent trees. His stomach felt emptier than ever. His paws were sore and blistered. The blows from the tomahawk had made his head swell and ache.

"Curse that Great Rabbit and his tricks!" he snarled, "I'll catch him yet – and I won't let him fool me again!"

In the morning he was soon back on Great Rabbit's trail. On and on and after him he bounded; but although the scent was always fresh, he could never catch up with the trickster.

At nightfall he came to a camp which consisted of just two lonely wigwams. A beautiful young woman stepped out of one at the sound of Wildcat's footfall. She brought him bowls of tasty food and sweet, cold water to drink. Then, noticing the bump on his head, she went into the second wigwam, calling her father to bring herbs.

"He is a famous healer," she said.

The man who stepped out was charming and gentle. But this time, Wildcat was on his guard, suspicious.

"Don't touch me!" he hissed. "I know who you are! Look at how your hair sticks up on either side of your head: it looks just like a rabbit's ears."

"My son," said the medicine man calmly. "Have no fear of me. It is the custom amongst all the men of our tribe to wear our hair in such scalp-locks."

"Ohoh," replied Wildcat, scratching at the ground with extended claws. "But why is your nose split in the middle, just like a rabbit's?"

"My son, have pity on me. Yesterday I was busy with my hammer when a sliver of stone broke off, flew up and split my nose."

"Oh yes, oh yes?" Wildcat paced around, peering and sniffing. "Ahah, but look at the soles of your feet. They're all yellow, just like a rabbit's."

"My son, do you see these healing herbs I bring to you? Yesterday I prepared them by stamping on them until the juices ran. It is this which has stained my feet."

Wildcat let out a great sigh of relief. "Then heal me, father," he begged.

So the medicine man went to him and rubbed magic substances deep into his wound. At once, Wildcat drifted off into a long, soothing sleep.

But when he woke up, he found he had been tricked once again. The wigwams had gone, hunger had returned – and the medicine trickling down from the wound onto his face was nothing more than foul, disgusting rabbit droppings!

Oh starvation, oh rage! Wildcat let out a savage scream.

Seven gigantic leaps ahead of him, Great Rabbit heard it. He stopped still and felt the magic throbbing through him. Aaah . . . he was weakening. There was only enough left for one more illusion. He must make it his most brilliant one yet.

He came to a lake and crossed to the far shore; then he threw a huge pawful of woodchips out across the bank.

At once the woodchips sprung up into an army of tall, fierce warriors. Row upon row, they tensed and waited. Their faces were bright with gleaming streaks of war-paint; huge crests of eagle feathers crowned their heads. Their strong hands gripped clubs and knives, bows and arrows, magic charms and every other imaginable weapon. Their deep voices chanted:

"Wildcat -
Kill him, kill him!
Scalp, scalp, scalp!"

At their head stood the warrior chief. His straight, furry ears were so long, they almost touched the Sky.

And now, here came Wildcat. Creeping, cringing, pacing, pouncing, he reached the lake's nearest shore.

"Hey Rabbit!" he yelled. "I know it's you! I'm not afraid! This army you're trying to terrify me with – it's only a stupid illusion!"

Then he plunged into the lake and began to swim straight towards the warriors.

"I'm coming to get you, Rabbit! This time you won't escape me. I'm going to tear you to pieces and gobble you up!"

Great Rabbit gave a single piercing shriek. At once the warriors hurled their weapons: clubs, spears, tomahawks, knives and arrows rained upon Wildcat from every side.

Oh, he knew it was only a game of magic, he knew it was only a trick of Great Rabbit's mind. He knew that at any moment Great Rabbit would blink and the warriors would fade away into thin air . . .

Yet just the same, magic can hurt, magic is powerful, magic might be deadly. Wildcat couldn't bear pain. Worse than that, he was scared, scared, scared.

So he leaped back out of the water, he turned and he ran – *scat!* – right away from Great Rabbit and his army, just as fast as he could.

Great Rabbit gave one last laugh and *wumph!* – at once his army of warriors was gone!

But Wildcat, he kept on running and running and running. He was too afraid to stop.

Well – and if he hasn't died yet, to this very day he must be running still.

The Man
Who Changed

Once there were two young men who ached with longing to know what lay beyond the edge of the world.

At last, one said,

"Something is calling me. Tomorrow I shall start to walk across the prairie until I come to the place where the grass and the singing wind circle up to meet the sky. Then I shall see what there is to see."

"Let me travel with you," said his friend. "If there are dangers to face or miracles to watch, we can share them together like brothers. I too have had dreams: we are fated to walk the same path."

So for many days they trudged together towards the South; yet however far they went, the horizon always seemed to slip away.

As they walked, they hunted for food. At first there was plenty; but soon the great plains grew quiet and utterly empty, until there was no more game to catch. Then hunger gnawed at their bellies.

"Father, send us something to eat!" they cried to the Sun.

Suddenly, through the vast sea of rippling grasses, they saw something white and gleaming.

They crept closer. Before them lay two enormous white eggs.

"Look," whispered the first man, "our prayer is answered!"

But the other shook his head.

"I have never seen eggs like this before. Perhaps they are poison. Perhaps they are dangerous magic. I would rather starve than eat them."

The first man hesitated. He bent to examine the eggs, running his hands gently over the smooth white shells, listening, thinking.

At last he stood up.

"You are wise to be cautious," he said, "but my heart tells me that these eggs have been placed in our path for a purpose. I shall taste them:

my brother, I am not afraid."

Dusk was falling. They gathered dried buffalo dung to build a fire and laid out their blankets, ready for sleep.

When the fire had settled to red, glowing embers in the darkness, the first man took the eggs and set them to roast. Then he cracked them open.

"Taste one," he offered. "They are sweet and rich."

But the other was still fearful, so the first man ate them both.

They slept until sunrise, then rolled up their blankets and walked on.

Very soon, the one who had eaten the eggs began to sway and stumble.

"You are ill," said his friend. "Those eggs have been quick to poison you with their evil magic. Perhaps we should turn back."

"No," said the other. "I am not ill; but I am changing. The eggs are magic indeed; but it is good. I must not – I cannot – go back. The Great Mystery is calling. I must follow where I am led until I find my home."

"Your words are strange and your eyes are strange," said his friend. "Yet we have sworn to be brothers. If you are strong enough to go on, I will respect your longing and walk with you."

Thus, silencing the fear in their hearts, they went on with their journey.

At midday they stopped to rest and dozed off under the hot Sun. When they woke, the one who had eaten the eggs found his skin had turned dry and scaly, etched with curious patterns. He stared at himself, then stretched and stood up.

But his legs could scarcely move, and would not support his weight: they felt stiff and heavy.

At once his friend was beside him, hunting for healing herbs inside his bundle.

"No, no, I am not ill. Don't be afraid my brother. The change is pouring through me now. When it is complete, I shall feel better – and you will understand."

"Then tell me what I can do to help you," begged his friend.

"Support me until I can no longer walk; and when that moment comes, slow your pace to mine. For then I shall have to crawl with my body pressed close to our Mother, the Earth. Brother, I beg you to stay by my side until I reach my journey's end."

"I swear to do all that you ask. But can you tell me yet where we are going?"

"On and on to the Winding Water; I shall know my place when I find it."

So they went on. At first the man who was changing managed to stumble along, leaning his weight on his friend's shoulders; but by the end of the day his legs had grown so heavy that all he could do was crawl and slither along the ground. His friend went ahead, opening a path for him through the tall, damp grasses, seeking a place to rest by the crimson-gold light of the setting sun.

At last they came to a small lake. The friend made a fire and used his bow to shoot down some small rabbits. While he was cooking them, the man who was changing plunged into the lake for a swim. He stayed in the water, splashing and diving until the meal was ready. As he slithered up the bank to share it, he smiled at the wonder in his friend's eyes.

"Brother – what has happened to you?!"

"It is almost finished. I feel good – better than I have ever done before!"

"But . . . what *are* you?"

The man who was changing looked down at his glistening wet body. His legs were gone, fused into a single long, powerful tail. His hands and arms were shrivelled away. The scales that covered his skin shone in the firelight, a patchwork of magic and patterns. Only his face still resembled what he had been before.

"I am a snake," he said softly.

"So! – What I see is not a vision?"

"Brother, your eyes show the truth. Yet still, I am also a man. Listen: now I know that snake and man are One and the same, two shifting shades of the Great Mystery's breath."

His friend bowed his head. "And tell me, what will happen next?"

"We will eat and we will sleep. In the morning I will travel further until I find my home in the Winding Water."

"And what of me?"

"Please – stay with me."

In the morning they went on. Now the man who had changed slid and writhed along the ground exactly like a snake, so that they could go a little quicker. In this way they continued their journey, stopping to eat and rest as they needed to, always seeking lakes or rivers where the snake-man could swim and build on his strength.

At last, on the fourth sunset after he had eaten the eggs, they came to a wide, winding river. At once the man who had changed cried out, "I am home!" and plunged in.

Darkness fell and the owls screeched. All night long he stayed hidden under water while his friend paced the bank, chanting softly and waiting.

Morning came. The surface of the water broke. He rose from the water a gleaming, great horned serpent: the Change was complete.

His friend stood awestruck on the bank. Then he found a voice to greet him.

"Though your shape is new, you are still my friend, my brother!" he called. "I am glad to have shared your fate with you."

The snake-man shook his magnificent head and flashed his forked tongue.

"You have helped me beyond thanks," he replied. "Now I long to help others in the same way. I beg you, do one more thing: go back to our people and say what has happened. Tell them what I have become: I am Guardian of the Lakes and Rivers.

"If they believe in me, let them bring gifts of food whenever they need to cross the water. Then, with the Great Mystery's blessing, I promise always to keep them safe."

And so it was. The other man went home, sad to be parted from his friend, but proud to tell his story. His people listened carefully.

Since then, they have always made offerings to the sacred Snake-Man whenever they come to water.

The Secret World
of the Ravens

Back through the memories of a thousand grandmothers lay a time when the world was new and there was nothing to eat but seeds and berries. Oh, the people were hungry!

There was a family who had built their hut right on the edge of the village. One morning the mother and father went out to search for food, leaving their four children to guard the fire.

Thus the children waited. And by and by, they heard someone knocking on the side of the hut. The door opened and in walked an enormous raven.

The raven was carrying a bow and a quiver. He put them down in a corner of the hut. Then, without a word, he hurried out and disappeared into the blue morning.

"Who? . . . What? . . ."

"Perhaps he has brought us a gift," whispered the eldest girl.

So they all crept over to see.

"Look inside the quiver."

"Whatever is it?"

"It smells like something to eat."

"Taste it then!"

The youngest boy broke off a small piece and put it into his mouth.

"Mmm, it's good!"

So all the children began to eat.

"Delicious!"

"Wonderful!"

"I've never felt so full!"

They were still enjoying the feast when their parents came staggering home. They both looked very weary, very worn; yet all they had brought back was a meagre half-basket of wild seeds to cook for supper.

When they saw their children, they cried out in astonishment.

"What magical change has come over you?"

For it was true: the two girls and two boys seemed suddenly to have grown sturdier, stronger, taller.

"A raven brought us this food," they replied.

Their parents tried it and within moments they too seemed to grow and change.

The whole family was singing with excitement. They ran out through the village, calling and shouting their news.

Then they took what remained of the marvellous food to show their Chief. The Chief tasted it: he sighed and smiled, savouring it with half-closed eyes.

"I have often dreamed of this," he said at last. "It is meat. It is what we need to banish hunger, to make our people for ever strong. The raven has brought it to us as a sign. We must follow him to learn where it comes from, and get some for ourselves."

So he sent out scouts, to seek the raven. But before long they came back, shaking their heads:

"The great bird was seen flying far, far away to the eastern mountains. There are more trails that lead that way than stars in the Sky. We will never find him."

Night fell. The Chief was sitting alone. A bat came to him, flying on silent wings.

"I have succeeded in following the raven!" it whispered. "I know the way to his secret world. If you are not afraid to travel in darkness, come with me. Bring all your people. Tell them, even the children, this: Be brave. Follow the path that is made. Act with care and wisdom. This way, in the end, you may all get what you most desire."

So the Chief led the people on a long, long journey. Following the bat, they walked through four dark nights towards the dawn.

At last they came to a tree place, high in the mountains, and here they stopped. The air was full of ravens, swooping, shrieking; and the ground was soft with layer upon layer of pine needles, the fallings of countless winters.

The people hid amongst the pine trees. They watched the ravens for a long time, bravely, patiently. But they learned nothing.

So at last their Chief called to the boy who had been the first to taste the wonderful meat.

"It is time to reveal ourselves," he said. "I choose you, boy. You must be the first to walk openly amongst the ravens. Seek out the great one who visited you, for he is surely their chief. Offer him my peace-pipe. Then you must beg him to show us the source of their magic food."

The boy was very frightened. How would he ever know which of the great black birds was the one? Slowly, trembling, he walked out into the raven place, holding the Chief's pipe aloft.

At once the Raven-Chief himself alighted on the ground before him!

"My son," he said, "I am happy that you have come."

The Raven-Chief took the pipe from the boy and breathed a flame to it; then he smoked it, seven times. First he smoked it to the four corners of the world: North, South, East, West. Then he smoked it to Father Sky above and to Mother Earth below. Lastly, he blew a puff to the very spot where the two of them stood.

After this, with a soft touch of his dark wing, he turned the boy into a puppy.

"You will stay here for a while," said the Raven-Chief, "but your people must go home."

The boy-puppy had no choice but to trust to fate. He crouched and watched and listened. Now the Raven-Chief called out to all the people,

"Come out from the corners where you hide! You are not needed here. Go back to where you come from: be patient and wait."

So the Chief led the people back home through the mountains. But the boy-puppy stayed amongst the ravens, alone.

Very soon, a raven-boy came along. When he saw the puppy, he called to it. They began to play together, chasing and tumbling on the soft ground.

Darkness came and the raven-boy took the boy-puppy home with him. The boy-puppy watched the raven family prepare for supper, but he could not see any sign of food.

Then the raven-father went to the fire that burned in the centre of the hut. Carefully, he brushed away a heap of ashes that had fallen from it. Underneath was a large, flat stone. Next, he lifted up the stone.

Underneath was a black, empty hole.

The raven-father stepped into the hole and disappeared.

Everyone waited and a little while later, he came back. Behind him was an enormous animal. The boy-puppy had never seen anything like it before. It was a buffalo!

The whole family gathered round excitedly as the father slaughtered the beast with his stone knife. They roasted its meat in the fire: how good it smelt! They ate, and threw scraps to the puppy: the meat tasted good too.

The boy-puppy stayed with the raven family for three days. Each evening the father disappeared under the stone in the same way and returned home with another buffalo to eat.

On the fourth morning the ravens left him alone inside the hut. Suddenly his body began to shake and quiver. He looked down at himself and found he had turned back into a boy!

"It is surely a sign," he said to himself. "On this, the fourth day, I must go under the stone, to the place where no person has ever been before."

He went to the fire and swept away the pale ashes. Beside them, he found a white eagle's feather. Taking this in his hand, silently, fearfully, he pushed up the stone.

Dark and deep was the hole. He held his breath and dropped down into it . . .

And down.

And down.

And down . . .

At last: the bottom – solid ground!

The darkness had gone. He was in a wondrous, beautiful world. Rich green grass stretched away to the four horizons, broken only by shimmering blue lakes. And everywhere he looked, near and far, herds of buffalo were grazing, like a great, dark murmuring sea.

The boy went up to a buffalo. He offered it the eagle feather. It gazed down at him and shook its head.

"No, no, not me," it said. "You must walk much further amongst my sisters and my brothers. At last you will come upon one who is as white as milk. He is our Chief. He is sacred. He alone can grant what you long for."

The boy wandered on and on, losing himself in the dark herd. The buffalo towered massive and strong above him, making him feel like a tiny ant.

Deep in their very centre, the sacred white Buffalo-Chief was watching him come. The boy was drawn to him. When he saw him, he gave a cry and held out the eagle's feather; and the white one took it.

"I welcome you, Son of the People," he said. "Now you must take us to your own land and make us welcome too. Lead, for we will follow."

So the boy turned and walked back. He led the way up through the hole, back to the Ravens' Land. Behind him came the white Buffalo-Chief, leading all the other buffalo.

From there he led them home, through the mountains, to the Land of People.

As soon as they arrived, the buffalo scattered over the wide earth. Now, whenever the people were hungry, the buffalo gave themselves up gladly to be killed for meat.

Since then, people have always eaten meat. That is why, of all Earth's creatures, we are the strongest and most powerful!

But whenever we kill a buffalo, we always leave the eyes for the ravens. May the winds carry our thanks to them, far in the distant mountains! Dark the birds, and dark the beasts that feed us: so we tell this tale and remember.

And that is all.

About the People
Who Told these Stories

Who are the Native Americans?

The Native Americans – also known as 'American Indians' or 'First Nations' – are the original inhabitants of Canada and the USA. They have lived there for at least 12,000 years, and possibly much longer.

There are several hundred different Native American tribes. Each tribe speaks its own language or dialect and follows its own customs. Each one also has its own name for itself: many of these names simply mean 'The People'. (The name 'Indian' was given by European explorers because when they first reached the American coast they mistakenly believed they were in India.)

How did they live when these stories were first told?

North America is a vast continent full of contrasts, extending from the frozen Arctic in the far north to the sub-tropical swamps of the deep south. There are deserts and lush forests, vast areas of flat grasslands and ranges of towering mountains.

The traditional way of life of each tribe depended very much upon the local landscape and climate. Some tribes lived mainly by farming, growing maize, beans, vegetables and fruit. Others were hunters and gatherers of wild food. Along the coasts, many people lived mainly by fishing.

All tribes were very skilled at craftwork and made everything that they needed themselves: houses, clothing, tools and utensils. These were often beautifully decorated with painted or carved designs, beads, feathers or porcupine quills.

Children were brought up firmly but with a lot of affection. They were

There are several hundred Native American tribes. This map shows the tribes whose stories are included in this book.

often looked after by their grandmothers: older people were treated with much respect. From an early age, both boys and girls began to practise the skills they would need as adults. They learned about their people's history, religions, laws and customs by listening to the elders' stories and by watching and participating in festivals and ceremonies.

About the tribes in this book

The tribes whose stories are featured in this book are shown on the map on page 90.

Horses and buffalo

The **Blackfeet** (stories on pages 9 and 69) and the **Cheyenne** (stories on pages 21 and 80) were two tribes of the Great Plains, a vast region of wide grasslands where millions of wild buffalo once roamed. They were nomadic people (regularly moving their homes from place to place), so lived in *tipis* – tents covered in animal hides, which were easy to put up and down and to carry about. The men hunted buffalo and other wild animals, whilst the women gathered wild plants for food. They were expert riders (horses were introduced to America by European invaders), and they frequently conducted wars and raids against neighbouring tribes in order to capture more horses.

The **Slavey** (story on page 30) had a similar way of life, although their home was further north in the harsh sub-arctic region of Canada. They lived by fishing, and by hunting and trapping wild animals.

Fishing and feasting

The **Tlingit** (story on page 16) lived along the coast and on the islands of south-eastern Alaska. They obtained almost all their food from the sea, fishing from dug-out canoes. They lived in villages of large, rectangular, wooden houses. The women wove beautiful blankets and baskets, whilst the men were brilliant sculptors and carvers.

The Tlingit often went to war with neighbouring people in order to capture slaves and to steal precious goods. Their leaders would later give these goods away as gifts to show off their wealth at ceremonial *potlatch* feasts.

91

Longhouses and wigwams

The **Iroquois** (story on page 25) and the **Algonquians** (story on page 75) came from the north-east region around the Great Lakes and the east coast, where the borders of the modern USA and Canada meet. Both were actually groups of several smaller tribes. The Iroquois were also known as the 'Six Nations'.

The Iroquois were farmers and fishermen. They lived in bark-covered longhouses, grouped together to form small towns. Inside each longhouse, between five and twenty individual families lived in their own apartments, whilst the central area was used as a communal meeting place. The Iroquois chiefs were men, but they were chosen by women, who also could get rid of any chief who did his job badly.

The Algonquian story belongs to the **Micmac** and **Passamaquoddy** peoples who lived amongst thick forests, rivers and lakes and also along the coast. They obtained food by fishing and hunting, travelling in birch canoes. They lived in *wigwams* – conical huts covered in birch-bark or woven mats.

People of the Pueblos

The **Tewa** (story on page 37), the **Hopi** (stories on pages 39, 45, 51 and 59) and the **Zuni** (story on page 61) lived in the south-west region of the USA and are known as 'pueblo Indians' or 'village dwellers'. Their traditional villages – still lived in today – consisted of small houses of stone and *adobe* (sun-dried brick) with several rooms, usually built by women. The centre of the village was the *kiva*, an underground chamber where religious ceremonies were performed. Pueblo life centred around the family and religion.

The climate in the south-west is hot with very little rain: despite this, the people were successful farmers who grew corn, beans, pumpkins and fruit.

Dome-shaped Houses

Also in the south-western region lived the **Pima** (story on page 55), who shared many of the pueblo peoples' love of peace. They lived in villages where each family had its own dome-shaped house made of wattle-and-daub. Their village chiefs and councils were chosen by election. They were farmers, using river water to irrigate their crops, which included tobacco and cotton as well as food. The Pima women were also famed for making beautiful baskets.

Other inhabitants of this south-western region were the **Jicarilla Apache** (story on page 84), one of the six nomadic Apache tribes. They lived mainly by hunting and gathering wild food, but also did some farming. The women were responsible for building their 'wickiup' houses (dome-shaped huts made of branches) and they also had considerable power within their families and communities. The men were fierce warriors, skilled horsemen and brilliant long-distance runners.

Acorns and furs

The **Yurok** (stories on pages 57 and 64) inhabited fifty small villages in what is now the state of California. They lived by fishing, hunting and gathering wild food: their most important foods were salmon and acorns. Life centred around the family, for they had no chiefs or formal leaders. They took great pride in being rich: they used money in the form of shells, furs and woodpecker scalps.

What religion did the Native Americans follow?

Each tribe had its own religion, but all shared certain basic ideas. They respected all the forces of nature and believed that everything in the world has a spirit: animals, plants, even rocks and water. Amongst some tribes the Sun, Moon and particular stars were important, and many revered Mother Earth as the source of all life. There was widespread belief in 'The Great Mystery' – an overall but abstract power controlling all the forces of creation and nature.

'Medicine men' – or sometimes women – were highly respected people who could communicate with the world of spirits, advise on the future, heal the sick and perform special sacred rituals. Magic was accepted as a normal part of existence. Songs, dances, private rituals and public ceremonies were regularly performed in the belief that they could magically influence events. 'Medicine' bundles' were treasured collections of ancient and sacred objects believed to bring protection and good luck.

What happened to the old Native American civilisations?

The Native Americans' way of life came under attack from the late 15th century, when the first European explorers reached the American continent. For the next 400 years, the people suffered greatly. Their land was seized by European settlers. In warfare, their bows and arrows were defeated by the more powerful guns of the 'White Man'. They died in huge numbers from European diseases such as measles and smallpox. Perhaps worst of all, the new settlers destroyed much of the natural environment and exterminated many of the wild creatures upon which the people depended.

By the end of the 19th century, most of the surviving Native Americans had been sent to live on 'reservations'. Here the land was often poor and they found it difficult to use their traditional skills. Their children were sent away to school and taught to adopt the new European-style culture. Despite this, many native American people took care to ensure that their customs and beliefs did not die out.

Is Native American culture still alive today?

Today there are about one and a half million Native Americans living in the USA, and nearly 300,000 in Canada. Some groups – such as the Hopi – still keep up their ancestral traditions, and Native Americans everywhere are increasingly proud to revive their rich cultural heritage, including languages, religious ceremonies, arts, crafts and story-telling.

Native American stories have much to teach the modern world with all its machines and pollution, conflict and uncertainty. They speak of a lost time when the whole of creation lived in harmony, when the Earth was treated with respect and the animals were our equals. They tell of people who were brave and loyal and did not give up easily, however difficult the task. But, above all, they are marvellous adventures.

SOURCES

L. H. Appleton, *American Indian Design and Decoration* (Dover Publications, New York 1971)

E. E. Clark, *Indian Legends of Canada* (McLelland & Steward, Toronto 1960)

H. P. Corser, *Totem Lore of the Alaska Indians* (The Nugget Shop, Juneau, Alaska, undated)

R. Erdoes & A. Ortiz, *American Indian Myths and Legends* (Pantheon Books, New York 1984)

A. L. Kroeber, *Yurok Myths* (University of California Press, 1976)

M. Leach (ed.), *Funk and Wagnalls Standard Dictionary of Folklore, Mythology and Legend* (New English Library, 1972)

M. Littman, *The People: Sky Lore of the American Indian* (Hansen Planetarium, Salt Lake City, Utah, 1976)

A. Marriot & C. K. Rachlin, *American Indian Mythology* (Thomas Y. Crowell Co., New York 1968)

G. M. Mullett, *Spider Woman Stories: Legends of the Hopi Indians* (University of Arizona Press, 1979)

L. Spence, *North American Indians: Myths and Legends* (George G. Harrap & Co., London 1914)

S. Thomson, *Tales of the North American Indians* (Indiana University Press, 1929)